THE NEW WORLD LANDSCAPES OF OEHME AND VAN SWEDEN
WOLFGANG OEHME JAMES VAN SWEDEN WITH SUSAN RADEMACHER

BOLD ROMANTIC
GARDENS

SPACEMAKER PRESS

Revised and reprinted 1998.

Spacemaker Press
602 E Street NE
Washington, DC 20002

Library of Congress Cataloging-in-Publication Data
Oehme, Wolfgang, 1930–
    Bold romantic gardens: the New World landscapes of Oehme and van Sweden/Wolfgang Oehme, James van Sweden, Susan Rademacher.
    p. cm
    Includes bibliographical references,
    ISBN 1-888931-10-8
    1. Landscape gardening. 2. Gardens—United States. 3. Gardens, American. 4. Plants, Ornamental—United States. 5. Oehme, Wolfgang, 1930– . 6. van Sweden, James, 1935– .
I. van Sweden, James, 1935– . II. Rademacher, Susan, 1954– . III. Title.
SB473.044   1990   90-81
712'.0973—dc2OCIP

Art Director and Book Designer – Kathleen K. Cunningham
Graphic Artist – Penelope Kriese

Principal photographer – Michael McKinley

Page 1: The Sheffield Garden in summer. Photograph by Bradley Olman.
Pages 2-3: The Offutt Garden in late summer. Photograph by Michael McKinley

Page 4: The Shockey Garden in summer. Photograph by Michael McKinley.

Calligrapher – Julian Waters
Architectural lettering – Lisa E. Delplace
Copy editor – Franziska Reed Huxley

Printed in Hong Kong

Books by James van Sweden

Gardening with Water (1995)
Gardening with Nature (1997)

To the memory of
Professor Jan Bijhouwer,
who brought us together

Table of Contents

Preface

The German-American Friendship Garden is a restful spot between the White House and the Washington Monument, on Constitution Avenue in Washington, D.C. Commemorating the 300th anniversary of German immigration to America, the garden features native plants of both countries. Two fountains of three jets each are designed like geysers erupting from the paving, so that people can walk right in and cool their feet. Photograph by Michael McKinley.

resh winds are astir in the field of American landscape design. They herald a dramatic break with our long-standing tradition of English park, estate and cottage garden.

Two free-spirited landscape architects, Wolfgang Oehme and James van Sweden, are introducing an exuberant approach uniquely suited to our times and the American temperament. They reject the "showcase" concept of the all-revealing lawn which extends from residence to the public street, advocating instead the creation of more private living spaces. They have eschewed the formal geometric patterns of the "grand plan" with its axial vistas, parterres, clipped hedges and topiary. They have avoided the platoon-like arboreal bosques within which the splendors of individual trees are lost in allegiance to the row or grid. Unlike anything yet seen in America, their designs avoid the meticulously manicured edgings and beds filled with plants spaced out in elaborate patterns.

In response to their freer approach, each plant seems to leap to life in an unrestrained display of foliage, flower, fruit and seedhead. Lush plantings of decorative grasses, bulbs and perennials are planned for year-round viewing. Trees may be massed as dark, free-form backdrops or placed to cast layers of delicate sunlit tracery over a pathway or space. They may be grouped in shadow-laced clusters, or perhaps a single specimen may be featured in silhouette against a pastel evening sky. Shrubs may be chosen for viewing in the round, clumped loosely, or strewn about in informal drifts. Perennial flowering plants are woven into luxuriant, verdant tapestries; annuals and vegetables may be set apart in containers. Ferns, mosses and succulents are selected and placed with infinite care to reveal the full beauty of their individual form, color and texture. Plant selection and placement—not only in relation to each other, but to just the right location, soil and exposure— are the keys to a garden that thrives with minimal care.

Consummate horticulturists, Oehme and van Sweden are *landscape architects* in the fullest sense of the word. Theirs is the art and science of creating out-of-door spaces. Such functional spaces may range in size from a child's play lot or kitchen herb garden to institutional grounds, urban parks, or the broad monumental sweep of avenues. Be it a homesite, shopping mall, or business office complex, each is conceived with care to express and fulfill its purpose. Each is planned to bring people and their activities into the best possible relationships with site features, views, the sweep of the sun, and the play of summer breezes. Each is designed outward to the far horizon and inward to the range of the user's full sensory perception.

In comprehensive land planning projects such as a parkway, campus or riverfront, Oehme and van Sweden may join teams of ecologists, economists, traffic engineers, and a panel of scientific advisors. Often, however, as in home and estate design, they join solely with the owners and architect to develop the plans and guide the work to completion.

Oehme and van Sweden are artists. Their designs are three-dimensional—created to be lived in, walked through, and enjoyed. The materials of their craft are ground forms, outcrops, water bodies and water courses, stone, gravels, soils, plants, and the whole range of fabricated wood, metal, concrete, ceramic, and other architectural products. With the broad landscape as base and backdrop, the earth plane is modeled and the space is enframed to bring structures, site development, and people into harmony with each other and the all-embracing landscape.

What are the distinguishing characteristics of Oehme and van Sweden landscape installations? Sometimes bold and exciting, sometimes subtle and serene, they are always vibrant and intensely alive. They are attuned to all seasons and hours of the day. In the gradual seasonal rotation, the more structural winter forms are softened by a fresh haze of budding foliage in the spring. Swaths of daffodils, tulips and crocus give way to the oncoming herbaceous perennials. In turn the more vivid hues of flowers and fruits succeed each other in ever-changing, free-flowing compositions. In late fall and through the winter, the taller grasses take over in shades of tawny rose, yellows, ochres, browns and copper. Trees and shrubs turn to sculpture. Such plantings are spontaneous, more natural, and far more satisfying than their traditional one-season counterparts. They seem to belong.

Another mark is the respect for fine architecture. Oehme and van Sweden bring buildings into sharper focus, with just the right, spare enframement. Gone are the familiar "foundation plantings" that hide a building's base, and the enveloping foliage that obscures clean architectural lines. Notable, too, is the imaginative use of water in jets, fountains, cascades or quiet reflecting ponds. Finally, Oehme and van Sweden have a way with light, revealing the constantly changing conditions of sunlight, shade and cast shadow. Their skillful use of evening illumination extends the hours of enjoyment and presents the garden landscape in a whole new way.

In our search for better cities and a more agreeable living environment we may take a clue from the innovative approaches of Oehme and van Sweden. These are engagingly described and superbly illustrated in the chapters which follow. Few readers will turn the last page of this handsome volume without an eager resolve to apply the creative ideas of these two landscape architects and their associates. In contemporary American garden design they are leading the way.

—John O. Simonds, F.A.S.L.A.

Foreword

*I*t is no wonder that the United States is still not recognized as a "gardening nation," when our traditional, green landscape consists of large shade trees and clipped evergreen foundation plants held together by the ruthlessly maintained lawn. "Color spots" are replanted every year according to our culture's "junk-it" mentality. Conversely, so-called "wild" gardens seldom live up to our images of nature because native plants are overwhelmed by exotic invaders and because we are largely ignorant of ecosystem management. Nature that is at once flourishing and predictable is rarely seen in our living spaces.

This bland and discouraging status quo need not continue, if we follow the progressive lead of Wolfgang Oehme and James van Sweden. Their gardens fulfill our dream of all-seasons display with a naturalistic balance of properly selected plants that thrive with a minimum of care. All plants are allowed within each growing season to expand to their full form without pruning, staking, deadheading or dividing. By fall the maturing seedheads, stalks, and leaves have embellished the entire garden space. They will continue to occupy the area until they are cut back just before the spring growth cycle begins again.

Oehme and van Sweden have opened our eyes to the beauty and utility of so many plants, such as *Eupatorium purpureum* 'Gateway' (Joe-Pye weed), which used to be absolutely forbidden in gardens. Wolfgang has a most unusual curiosity about new plants and is always looking for special introductions which we at the U.S. National Arboretum often bring to his attention. Oehme and van Sweden continue to build an interesting palette by never taking a plant for granted—progress continues to improve even the most familiar, favorite plants.

As their client for the New American Garden at the U.S. National Arboretum, I can enjoy observing a unique collaboration. James is strong on space and context,

A "Winter Garden Bouquet," picked from the New American Garden at the United States National Arboretum, contrasts the brilliant red berries of *Ilex verticillata* 'Sparkleberry' and raspberry-colored fruits of *Sorbus alnifolia* (mountain ash) with the subtle hues and textures of *Perovskia atriplicifolia, Miscanthus sinensis purpurascens,* and *Sedum* x *telephium* 'Autumn Joy', all set off by the foliage of *Magnolia grandiflora* (southern magnolia) and *Quercus rubra* (red oak). The arrangement by Dr. H. Marc Cathey is set among the National Capitol Columns, designed by EDAW, Landscape Architects, and the late Russell Page, designer. Photograph by Rhoda Baer.

whereas Wolfgang is strong on plants and associations, but when they plan and sketch together, each is demanding of the other to attain the most effective solution for the particular site. They always work within the reality of the land itself, taking responsibility in the field, fine-tuning the garden to its perfect pitch. *Bold Romantic Gardens* reveals the process Oehme and van Sweden use to analyze a site, the client's needs, and identify the technical problems that must be solved. The drawings presented in these pages show that their design principles apply in every region of this country; their plant lists are continually expanding as they design and build gardens in more and more locations.

In our throwaway society, where planned obsolescence extends even to plants, Oehme and van Sweden create "investment" gardens by bringing good horticultural practices into design. They pioneered the uniform treatment of an entire landscape as the garden, with soil preparation, watering and drainage systems throughout. Root systems can spread freely and plant performance is consistent across the garden. Unlike most new landscapes, these are not overplanted. The garden contains no throwaways and plant division is a rare chore. You'll find no hokey, theme gardens—no "white" gardens or wagon wheels. The only special elements are water features and sculpture, which show that clients consider the garden an investment.

Oehme and van Sweden are bringing changes to the green industry, too. Because they do not use mass-produced plants, a new auxiliary of speciality nurseries has developed to service their designs. In general, more and more perennials are being grown, treated as such, and planted in the fall. Before Oehme and van Sweden, perennials were treated like annuals: divided and planted in the spring, cut back after flowering, and ignored until the next spring. Americans often interfere with what nature rapidly restores. In our rush to be tidy, we forget that every plant has a failsafe system: it will produce seed or send out a volunteer shoot. Oehme and van Sweden's style is revolutionary in our youth culture, because they have shown us how beautiful is the entire life cycle of a plant. These gardens come into their own from August into December, when all around you nature is destroying itself in the annual cycle of senescence. Their gardens, after the first frost, enter a whole new stage of aged beauty.

Their style has revived the cutting garden, too. Annuals have been bred to be so short that you cannot use them as cut flowers anymore. (It is one of life's little ironies that I researched chemical growth retardants many years ago for the U.S. Department of Agriculture. Our goal was to eliminate staking, increase stress resistance and intensify leaf color.) But in the "Bold Romantic Garden," you can "steal branches" whether they are in bud, flower, deadhead or seed. There is always something to cut for that touch of hospitality on the kitchen table or in the guest room. Without destroying the overall effect, the whole garden becomes a cutting garden.

Plants moving in space with light—this is the first thing you see in an Oehme and van Sweden garden. The fluid foliage of ornamental grasses gives these gardens more movement and naturalism than we usually see in most uptight American landscape design. Now we are beginning to see look-alike gardens based on certain signature plants. But when you analyze the gardens of Oehme and van Sweden, it is not the plants themselves, but their interrelationships in space that is unexpected and so effective. This is plant association for aesthetics. It is critical to understanding how their gardens work.

Unlike typical landscape architecture, the visual emphasis is not on the benches, walks and walls of a garden "room." Their gardens do not define space as a room; the furniture is not fixed. A bench is placed wherever the garden is most beautiful at the moment. The "Bold Romantic Garden" is primarily to be viewed as you move through portals, around screens and through plants themselves. To really see the garden, you must look ahead and behind. Walks on all sides of the plants give you a chance to be involved with the total plant from every perspective. "Foundation planting" is no longer an appropriate word because all the garden is one integrated whole. Plants flow right to you and stop, as if you said, "Enough!"

These are profound innovations in using plants and looking at the landscape. As masters of horticulture and space, Wolfgang Oehme and James van Sweden have joined my short list of personal heroes. They bring revolutionary ideas to the American gardening scene that may yet earn our beautiful country the esteemed status of a gardening nation.

—Dr. H. Marc Cathey
Director
U.S. National Arboretum

Introduction

Being in this garden world is a romance of all the senses and the imagination. You are immersed among plants that reach across a path to touch you, eyestruck by the handsome spikes of *Acanthus hungaricus,* curiosity piqued by mysterious shadows, sculpture and lines of movement. The van Sweden Garden in early summer. Photograph by James van Sweden.

It has been eight years since *Bold Romantic Gardens: The New World Landscapes of Oehme and van Sweden* was published. We were a young company then, enjoying our first significant successes. We were developing a national reputation for reinvigorating the American garden and for liberating suburban properties from the tyrannies of the front lawn and garish annuals, using revolutionary planting and design techniques that were, ironically, as old as the garden itself.

Today we can appreciate the book's influences, not only on our own professional practice, but on the entire field of landscape architecture in this country and abroad. It has become a classic teaching and reference volume used by students and professors of landscape architecture at universities and colleges around the world.

How can we explain this degree of influence? Certainly, it is a beautiful book. The projects are gorgeously photographed and described. But *Bold Romantic Gardens* is more than a coffee-table book. In some ways, it is a subversive text: a chronicle of our methods for overturning outmoded approaches to landscape design and plantings, and a guide for bringing nature more fully into our lives.

Gardens depicted in this volume represent the defining moments of our partnership. These gardens show how our early risks of scale and vision paid off with striking results. As you will see, they provide the setting for a profound interplay of texture, color, scent, sound, and introduced elements—particularly water—that we maintain are essential to our well-being. They demonstrate how we both blur and strengthen the boundaries between public and private spaces. They also address our concerns for year-round interest and relatively easy care.

Rereading it, I'm struck both by how much the book still has to teach us, and by how far we've come in the last eight years. The early use of ornamental grasses and perennials that we proposed, the gorgeous audacity of our hardscape designs, Wolfgang's talent for "painting" with plants—each piece has contributed to the change in our national landscaping appetites.

With the publication of my two latest books, *Gardening with Water* and *Gardening with Nature*, we've gotten our message out to an even wider audience. We've tried to show how it's possible for anyone with a modest plot of earth and a little effort to perform alchemy, even in the tightest of spaces. A tiny urban lot can become a paradise. Thanks to the expansion of the garden-center industry, it's now easy to find the sorts of unusual plant materials that Wolfgang labored to introduce to this country thirty years ago.

Like any successful long-term partnership, ours has matured. Our stylistic differences—my volubility, Wolfgang's reserve—often have been remarked upon, and they continue to work to everyone's advantage. Our skills, we find, are complementary, and we still enjoy a good laugh now and then. From a partnership of two, working out of a bedroom in my townhouse in Washington, D.C., and later expanding to a small shop of five architects, our firm has tripled its staff. Despite the increase in our volume of work, Wolfgang and I continue to involve ourselves in each project from start to finish, and especially during the conceptual phases. But now we also spend more time spreading the word, teaching and lecturing to disseminate our ideas, much as one broadcasts seeds to create an abundant meadow tapestry.

Our projects have become more complex and varied. We've had the opportunity to build gardens around the world, from Germany to Argentina. And the nature of our work also has become more public. Among our 60 current projects we count two parks in Boston and a major urban redevelopment project in downtown Norfolk, Virginia. We're especially proud of one public project in particular: recently we won the "competition of the century" to design the new World War II memorial on the national mall in Washington, D.C.

Water features continue to be crucial elements of our designs. We're always coming up with innovative ways to introduce water into gardens of all sizes. We've also expanded the metaphor of the meadow by mixing perennials together and broadcasting them across the garden plane in an overall pattern, not just in clumps or groups. Finally, our hardscape has caught up with the sophistication of our planting design. We're using venerable materials, such as wood, stone, and concrete, in ingenious architectural ways.

We've also learned the importance of writing about and photographing our work. Gardens are ephemeral. They unfold in space and time, and by definition they are always evolving. Therefore we've made it an important part of our mission to capture all of our gardens' phases in still photographs, to chronicle their life cycles and displays. The winter garden truly is a different place from the midsummer or spring garden—it rebounds with its own wildlife, palette of colors, and music. By tracing the development of our gardens through language and image, we have attempted to fix them in our readers' minds.

We hope you enjoy reading—or rereading—*Bold Romantic Gardens* and that its images bring you that much closer to the pleasures of creating a garden of your own.

USING THIS BOOK

We have sought to make this an honest book that emphasizes image, since garden design is, after all, a visual art. The text is informally written to provide straightforward information. "Inspirations" reveals the layers of meaning in the title, *Bold Romantic Gardens*—an equilibrium of masculine and feminine, bold line and intricate detail, modern and picturesque styles. It shows how personal traits and historical influences interweave, leading to a partnership based on shared values and principles of design.

Next, Part II puts these principles into practice. An introductory essay discusses the fundamentals of design, followed by the "Anthology of Private and Public Gardens." We were delighted to discover that "anthology" comes from the Greek term for a collection of flowers, and we arranged this section as we would a bouquet, sprigged with cameo images from other gardens to emphasize or contrast with the fifteen featured gardens. The collection is unified by two criteria: that the gardens exemplify key design principles, and represent the range of our work to date.

Each of the fifteen featured gardens is explained through an ensemble of text, photographs, and drawings. An introductory essay describes the geographical and vernacular context, the opportunities and problems, and the design response. While this general text tells the story of each garden, captions describe how the design works in detail. A site plan shows the overall layout of spaces, somewhat like a map. In cases where the topography is significant, we provide a cross-section through the landscape to depict changes of grade. Within each garden, a planting design is featured in a paired photograph and silhouette drawing, keyed to a planting plan. The first and last gardens of the Anthology, both owned by devoted gardeners, show the qualities that result from ongoing design involvement.

Parts III and IV cover the specific principles and technical aspects that go into putting a garden together. A "Gallery of Built Elements" shows constructed details in photographs and drawings, cross-referenced where possible to the garden of origin. Similarly, most listings in the "Glossary of Favorite Plants" are cross-referenced to a photograph showing the plant in a garden context. Plants are always referred to by their botanical names, with common names given parenthetically in the case of plants not included in the Glossary. This ensures accurate selections for the garden, since common names vary wildly from place to place. With this kind of detailed information, we hope the book will be an instrument of study and inspiration for many years to come.

ORIGINS AND ACKNOWLEDGMENTS

In planning the book, we were inspired by the simple elegance of Thomas Church's *Gardens Are For People*, which presents the garden as a work of art arising from the needs of the client and the nature of the site. We are grateful to the many individuals who have encouraged and guided this project to fulfillment. Barbara Plumb was a true believer and introduced us to Mary Gilliatt, who tirelessly promoted the idea of a book. Jane Jordan, picture editor for Time-Life Books, taught us a great deal about garden photography, as have so many gifted photographers who have portrayed the gardens. One of the earliest photographers on the scene, William Dreyer must be especially acknowledged as the graphic artist who established the Oehme, van Sweden logo. Wordsmiths Andy Harney, Carole Ottesen, Linda Morris and Douglass Lea have helped to jell ideas over the years, while early versions of the outline were written by David Schaff and John Brookes. Thoughtful commentators on the final manuscript included Ewing Fahey, Dr. H. Marc Cathey, Nancy Watkins Denig, and Charles E. Turner. Jacqueline Heriteau provided sage advice on approaching publishers, and Benjamin Zelenko gave legal counsel.

Wolfgang remembers with appreciation the late Bruce Baetjer of Baltimore, who hired him on recommendation of the late Hubert Owens, dean of the school of environmental design, University of Georgia. Wolfgang is also grateful for the support of Dr. Richard Lighty, Thomas Michalski, Eckhardt Below and Friedrich Oehmichen. Walter Neumann, Dr. Hans Simon and Hermann Müssel provided essential horticultural contacts in Germany. Other key connections were made by Norman K. Johnson and by Anneliese Nassuth, who introduced me to Mien Ruys. Geraldine Schaddelee Holt graciously provided information and photographs of her family's garden. For unstinting support, we give heartfelt thanks to Shirley and Roland Oehme, Johanna van Sweden, Jonn H. Frey, Marilyn Melkonian, and Stanley and Claire Sherman.

We also recognize with high esteem the dedication, insights, and contributions of the professional staff of Oehme, van Sweden and Associates. In addition to their direct role in producing beautiful drawings, accurate research, and editorial comment, each has seen projects to fruition and supervised the maintenance of gardens over the years with complete professionalism. Also of great value has been the outstanding craftsmanship of stonemason James Birks; landscape contractor George Fossett; nurserymen Hammond Brandt, Kurt Bluemel, and Richard Simon; and swimming pool contractors Robert and Duncan McKeever. Thanks also to Sylvester March of the U.S. National Arboretum for horticultural advice.

Finally, Wolfgang and I wish to thank all the clients who have made these gardens possible. Among Wolfgang's earliest supporters in Baltimore were Leo and Pauline Vollmer, Bertram and Shirley Rice, Dr. Elliott and Marcia Harris, and Marjorie Crook. In Washington, D.C., early supporters were V. V. Harrison, John and Evelyn Nef, Barbara Woodward, Dr. Jerald and Barbara Littlefield, Jonathan and Arlinka Blair, and David and Perrin Lilly. All those who have supported us must be thanked for having had the courage to take a chance.

—James van Sweden

Part I

Inspirations

The Story of a Partnership

Curiosity brings us together. We have always looked beyond our own borders, both geographically and personally, opening our minds to learn how other people see and live. From shop windows to ancient shrines, the world's visual richness is thrilling. Even at mid-life, you can be overwhelmed by a culture's expression in every detail. Travel sparks creativity, as impressions are shared and percolate into our work.

Adventuring in design takes a certain stance: clear values, a willingness to confront our weaknesses, confidence in our strengths, and an appreciation for serendipity. The artistic life, like art itself, is open-ended. You arrive at unexpected places by unknown roads, and by letting go. We have found that rarest of creative visions—a true collaboration. We can allow each other free rein because we are secure in our individual contributions and respectful of each other's gifts. Always, we are refreshed by a dynamic meeting of the minds, based upon shared values and diverse experiences.

Opposite: Karl Foerster's own garden in Potsdam, Germany, exemplified his extraordinary, planterly approach to overall design. Layers of interesting plants—contrasting texture, shape, leaf sizes—create mystery that seduce the eye into the depths of the garden. He used plants boldly, both as a painting on the ground plane and as sculpture. Photograph, ca. 1930, courtesy of Marianne Foerster.

Preceding page: Garden wall at the entrance to the home of Roberto Burle Marx, Brasil. Photograph by James van Sweden.

WOLFGANG OEHME'S STORY

I was very interested in poetry and plays as a youngster. Along with Heinrich Heine and Johann Wolfgang von Goethe, Friedrich von Schiller was a favorite, probably because his writings on freedom and revolution appealed as I was growing up in an age of repression. It was the drama, the high moment of passion that I loved most of all. It called forth my imagination to dream.

World War II was a great upheaval for persons who loved plants and design. In Bitterfeld, Germany, everything had grown up in thickets due to wartime neglect, so there was much to do as I entered training. Apprenticeship in Max Illge's Bitterfeld nursery taught me trade skills like propagation and planting, with emphasis on annuals. Com-

Working as a student in Sweden, Wolfgang Oehme explored native habitats of the countryside. Photograph, 1953, by Rolf Schmidt.

mercial production was largely limited to fruits and vegetables because of food shortages after the war. Consequently, I did not learn about perennials until my first job with the Bitterfeld cemetery and parks department, which was permitted to grow its own ornamental plants for maintenance purposes.

That was when I decided to become a landscape architect. Hans Joachim Bauer, director of the department, profoundly influenced my direction. He is a landscape architect with vision, and he knows plants well. Together we went to other cities to look at plants, parks and botanical gardens. I soon concluded that it would be much better to design parks and large-scale projects than to remain within the limitations of nursery work. Nurseries are so demanding that you can not travel easily. Instead, I followed in Bauer's footsteps, studying for a degree in landscape architecture in Berlin, even though it meant leaving "East Germany" in 1952. With its fantastic botanical gardens, Berlin was the only place to be, the capital of the horticultural field. That is where I first saw ornamental grasses in extensive use.

Bauer had introduced me to the ideas of Karl Foerster (1874–1970) when I was still in Bitterfeld. Foerster's work was founded on movements in turn-of-the-century Germany which held that house and garden are intimately related, and which based landscape forms on ecological models and natural plant associations. Foerster's greatest contribution was in making plants central to the garden, especially the taller perennials, grasses, ferns and alpines.[1] A pacifist, Foerster linked the health of the world with gardens and advocated bringing gardens to all people. His public gardens and own nursery demonstrated the concept of *Durchgebluht,* or "bloom throughout" the year. These were gardens designed to be interesting in every season. He called them *Sichtungsgarten,* or "viewing gardens," and promoted the garden as a learning place.

Unlike most modernized cities,
Rothenburg ob der Tauber, Germany, is preserved
in its natural setting and represents, in one
sense, "the Old World that I escaped." This photograph
of Wolfgang was taken on his last visit with relatives
before emigrating to Baltimore, U.S.A., in 1957.
Photograph by Walter Neumann.

After World War II, outdoor garden exhibits were held throughout Germany as a way of reclaiming the devastated landscape. We were not building battleships anymore, so we could afford to build parks. As a student in Hamburg, I had the exhilarating experience of working for a "Bundesgartenschau," under the direction of chief landscape architect Karl Plomin. This national garden show transformed the whole city, and myself as well. Thousands of people came streaming through as we were still sweeping in the background. It gave me a vision of what plants can do for people. Plants need to be brought wherever people work; gardens are not just for weekends and holidays, they are for everyday life.

When I came to Baltimore, it was like a desert. I went on a crusade. People were very open to my ideas, but it was extremely difficult to find the variety of plants I wanted, especially grasses. I often resorted to digging unusual tree species, such as *Aralia spinosa,* in the woods, and hand-carrying seeds on return trips from Germany. With the arrival of German nurseryman Kurt Bluemel, the support of Wayside Gardens and Richard Simon at Bluemount Nurseries, and much detective work among the German network of designers and plantsmen in America, the supply slowly began to meet demand.

TIMELINE: WOLFGANG OEHME

1930	Born, Chemnitz, Germany
1950	Apprenticeship, Bitterfeld Horticultural School, Germany
1953	Planten und Blomen, Hamburg, Germany; Nursery work in Sweden
1954	Degree in Landscape Architecture, University of Berlin, Germany
1954-56	Nursery work in England; Parks Department, Frankfurt, Germany
1956-65	Delius Landscape Architects, Baltimore, Maryland; Bruce Baetjer, Landscape Architect, Baltimore, Maryland; Baltimore County (Maryland) Department of Recreation and Parks
1962-64	Faculty, Department of Landscape Architecture, University of Pennsylvania
1965	Faculty, Department of Landscape Architecture, University of Georgia
1966-74	Independent Practice, Baltimore, Maryland
1975	Principal and Cofounder, Oehme, van Sweden & Associates, Inc., Washington, D.C. Representative Commissions/Principal-in-Charge: Redesign of Pennsylvania Avenue planting from the U.S. Treasury to the National Gallery, Washington, D.C.; Virginia Avenue Gardens of the Federal Reserve, Washington, D.C.; Morrill Hall Gardens at the University of Minnesota, Minneapolis; U.S. Fish and Wildlife Service National Conservation Training Center, Shepherdstown, West Virginia; MacArthur Center retail complex in downtown Norfolk, Virginia; and projects in Chemnitz and Magdeburg, Germany
1987	Distinguished Service Award, Perennial Plant Association
1991	Elected to Fellowship in the American Society of Landscape Architects
1996	PROCESS: Architecture (#130): Wolfgang Oehme & James van Sweden: New World Landscapes, Process Architecture Co., Ltd., Tokyo, Japan

JAMES VAN SWEDEN'S STORY

As a boy, I was interested in gardens. I enjoyed taking care of flower borders at home and hated cutting the lawn. Although my parents did not garden, I was profoundly affected by winter visits to the Schaddelee Estate in Fort Myers, Florida. I loved this 'Twenties-era formal garden with its long axis extending out on a pier in the Caloosahatchie River, and its looser side gardens with sunset viewing kiosks. In Michigan, my Grand Rapids neighbors' more modest efforts inspired me, too. Across the street, Mrs. Smith's beautiful border of *Iris, Echinops* and *Phlox* gradually took over the shrinking lawn. Margaret Holmes, who is still my dear friend, was a wonderful gardener, a lover of the meadow and wild flowers, a teacher and a counselor who directed me toward architecture. Although my great-grandfather was an architect, and I always had summer jobs in the family contracting business, my parents never pressured me to become an architect.

At Wheaton College I pursued the liberal arts. I played cello in the orchestra, loved art classes and did a lot of painting. Two courses changed me forever. "The History of Civilization" showed the importance of architecture in the whole fabric of civilization. I had never before thought of architecture in a philosophical way. "Art Appreciation" brought out the artist in me and showed architecture's relation to all other arts.[2]

Approach to the boat basin at the Schaddelee Estate, Fort Myers, Florida. Photograph, ca. 1925, courtesy of Geraldine Schaddelee Holt.

Above: The "outdoor room," as the 17th-century Dutch knew it, was a walled town garden, comfortable and cozy, but also relating to the greater cityscape with glimpses of neighboring roofs and the new church tower on the main square of the city of Delft. This painting says everything about proportion and composition; diagonal lines lead the eye through the painting, not unlike the leading lines in three-dimensional garden composition. Pieter de Hooch (1629-ca. 1684). *A Dutch Courtyard.* Ca. 1656. (26¾" × 23") Mellon Collection, National Gallery of Art, Washington, D.C.

Opposite: Helen Frankenthaler places great washes of color in cloud-like forms on the canvas, the viewer looks deeply into the heart of space, filled with movement. Such a painting may be seen as a kind of symbol for the perennial meadow garden, dealing with the entire area as one composition that moves beyond the frame. Helen Frankenthaler. *Nature Abhors a Vacuum.* 1973. Acrylic on canvas. 8'7½" × 9'4½". Private collection, Andre Emmerich Gallery, New York.

In five years of studying architecture at the University of Michigan, I was most excited by designing a theoretical new town. At last the light went on: my true interest was in the space between buildings, not buildings themselves. My professors thought the only way to learn such a nebulous field was to study landscape architecture. Fortunately, Professors Charles Cares, Walter Chambers and William Johnson had just come to the University of Michigan to give new life to the department of landscape architecture. William Johnson was an especially great influence, teaching proportion and a rational approach to design and analysis. After receiving my degree in architecture, I was advised to go to the Netherlands to seek my Dutch roots and study urban space, especially since the Dutch had been planning cities since the Middle Ages.

World War II's devastation provided tremendous opportunities for city planning in Europe; leading planners, in the spirit of the pre-war *avant garde,* were determined to break away from the past. My romantic idea to study the proportions of old town squares was promptly dashed by Professor Cor van Eesteren, a planning professor at the University at Delft, head of Amsterdam's planning office for many years, and a founder of the De Stilj movement. He said, "Oh! These old-fashioned places are a big nuisance. We should get rid of it all. Nothing should hold us back." To hear such a shocking thing as a young man of 25 was unforgettable.

Another professor, Jan Bijhouwer, led a town planning movement that advocated social concerns, coinciding with a more natural approach to design. He believed in the evolution of a place, and actually planted projects without paths, letting people move across the landscape as they desired, and then paving the walkways wherever the "cow paths" formed. Now considered to be the Twentieth Century's most important Dutch landscape architect, Professor Bijhouwer planted the reclaimed land of the polders.[3] It was my privilege to work with him on the design of a greenbelt between Amsterdam and Rotterdam. Professor Bijhouwer introduced me to garden design on a big scale. On my return to the United States, he provided an introduction to Wolfgang Oehme. At that time, however, I was interested in building cities, not gardens as such, so I went to work in city planning.

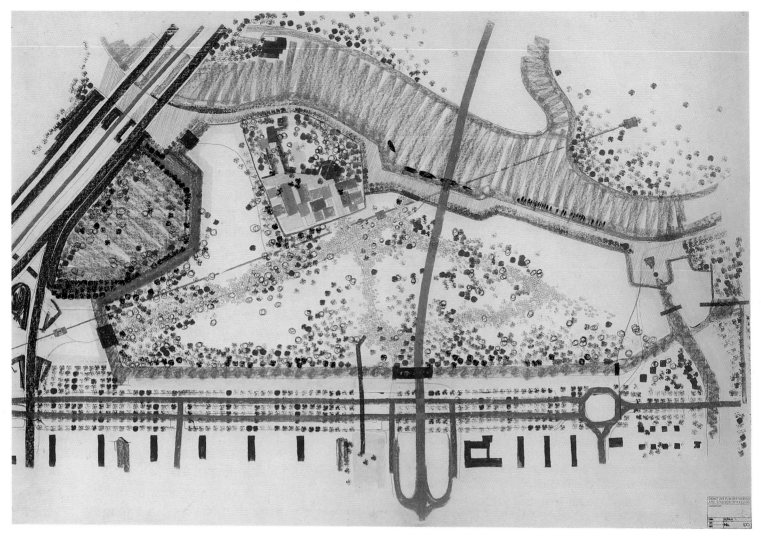

A 1961 drawing by James van Sweden of the Floriade exhibition grounds on the Amstel River, Amsterdam, The Netherlands, designed with Siegfried Nassuth in the Department of Public Works. The park's design included a riverside esplanade and a harbor for boats from the center of the city, while incorporating a historic residence and windmill. Pastel with India ink.

Despite the stimulation of working with George T. Marcou and Jeremiah D. O'Leary Jr., thirteen years in the ambiguous field of city planning was disappointing. For true city planners and urban designers, process is an end in itself. For the son of a builder, it was not enough. I had to see results. I didn't care if it was the tiniest private garden. I never dreamed of working at the urban scale of Battery Park City on Manhattan or Lincoln Park Zoo in Chicago—happily bringing me back full circle to what I wanted to do in the first place—design the space between buildings.

TIMELINE: JAMES ANTHONY VAN SWEDEN

1935	Born, Grand Rapids, Michigan
1960	Bachelor of Architecture, University of Michigan
1961	Graduate Studies in Landscape Architecture and Urban Design, University of Michigan and University at Delft, The Netherlands
1961-63	Assistant Town Planner, Amsterdam Planning Office, The Netherlands
1964-74	Partner in Charge of Urban Design and Landscape Architecture, Marcou, O'Leary and Associates, Washington, D.C.
1975	Principal and Cofounder, Oehme, van Sweden & Associates, Inc., Washington, D.C. Representative Commissions/Principal-in-Charge: Charles River Basin master planning and parks design, Boston, Massachusetts; Francis Scott Key Memorial Park, Georgetown, Washington, D.C.; Frederik Meijer/Michigan Botanic Gardens, Grand Rapids, Michigan; International Center embassy campus for the U.S. Department of State, Washington, D.C.; Nelson A. Rockefeller Park on the Hudson River, New York City; Red Butte Garden and Arboretum Rose Garden, Salt Lake City, Utah; and the proposed World War II Memorial on the National Mall, Washington, D.C.
1983, 87, 92	Study visits to Japan
1986	Joined Faculty, La Napoule Landscape Design Program, Cannes, France
1987	Thomas Roland Gold Medal, Massachusetts Horticultural Society
1992	Landscape Design Award, American Horticultural Society (jointly with Mr. Oehme)
1993	Elected to Fellowship in the American Society of Landscape Architects
1996	PROCESS: Architecture (#130): Wolfgang Oehme & James van Sweden: New World Landscapes, Process Architecture Co., Ltd., Tokyo, Japan

PARTNERSHIP

> "I'll never forget the moment I walked through the Vollmer's gate. I had never seen such a beautiful garden in all my life. I knew right then that Wolfgang Oehme was somebody to grapple with, to be involved with. And I waited 13 years."
>
> —*J.v.S.*

We met in 1964. Frequent visits over the ensuing decade strengthened our friendship until we finally designed a garden together. It was 1971, it was the van Sweden Garden, and it was a great success. People seemed to like it very much. By 1975, we were able to announce our partnership on the strength of that first project.

> "We wanted to explore how to do things differently."
>
> —*W.O.*

An American and a European, we immediately complemented each other in training and expertise. Together we covered the spectrum from architecture to city planning/urban design to landscape architecture to horticulture. Both of us had concentrated on public work in our early careers, but came to influence each other greatly in planting design and garden architecture. At first, architecture was relegated to the background in favor of plants; now our work is balanced, bringing the "bones" up to the level of the plants.

By the same token, our early drawings were very sketchy. The designs worked, because we built and planted the gardens ourselves and did a tremendous amount of adjustment in the field, just as gardeners do. We didn't have time to produce finished drawings. However, we couldn't avoid that in public work, with bidding and presentations to the National Commission of Fine Arts. Fortunately, our background in architecture and city planning firms—where presentation graphics are very important—has helped us to communicate our ideas.

Planting the early gardens ourselves brought us together in many ways. Through physical exertion, great enthusiasm, and learning from each other, we were like sculptors working as a team. It broke down all the barriers as we laughed a lot, learned costly lessons about drainage, and found out what very hard workers we both were. Our success as a team also owes a lot to luck based on instinct.

In 1982, Wolfgang Oehme, left, and James van Sweden together planted the prototype for a series of containers designed by Robert Venturi at Freedom Plaza, Pennsylvania Avenue, Washington, D.C. Photograph by Oehme, van Sweden & Associates.

We've been in the right place at the right time, made the right decisions, and had the privilege of working with very stimulating people, like Siegfried Nassuth in the Amsterdam city planning office, Jeremiah D. O'Leary Jr. and Hans Joachim Bauer.

Washington, D.C., was a challenging environment in which to start out. It offered a wonderful climate for gardens, yet it was stifled by a monumental and hot "hardscape," overlain with an equally boring, static "plantscape." The gardens had that plastic evergreen look: people were mad for azaleas, but there was painfully little interest on the ground plane. Fortunately, Washington and Baltimore clients tend to be very intelligent, daring people who want to make an impact. Americans in general like to make a statement, and having an exciting garden is one way to win recognition. Washingtonians like to entertain outside and with exercise in vogue, we like to say, "Don't jog, garden!" We have tried to satisfy the need for individual expression in an establishment town, and to overlay the monumental landscape with shade, movement and humor.

Our partnership truly began when we recognized in each other curious, sensitive people who could do something, especially together. We bounce ideas off each other, compare notes, shore up, and give whatever is needed. Although we are quite different in dealing with clients and expressing our ideas, the sum is definitely more than the parts. It lets us build our fantasies.

PRINCIPLES OF NATURALISM

If our work has sometimes been labeled "The New American Garden," we would define it as a kind of "melting pot" of international plants and ideas, producing an alloy of naturalism and free spirit.[4] We are inspired by the East and the West, by the historic and the contemporary, and especially by the work of such designers as Jens Jensen and Karl Foerster.

Jensen (1860–1951) was a Danish-born landscape architect who brought his attitude of living with nature's frame to the American Midwest. A friend of Frank Lloyd Wright, Jens Jensen developed a "Prairie Style" in landscape, known for compositions of native plants, and naturalistic rockwork. With great success in private properties and public parks, Jensen's work called forth our American nostalgia for open frontier and reverence for nature.

In the Netherlands, between the world wars, Mien Ruys (b. 1904) and others were inspired by the English team of Gertrude Jekyll and Edwin Lutyens to forego the 18th-century landscape style in favor of an architectural framework supporting perennial borders of large, informal drifts of color. It was a modern movement that embraced functionalism, architectural form and re-evaluated the English cottage garden. The designs of Ruys were strong in concept and detail, and have been greatly influential through design projects and demonstration designs at her family's renowned nursery (Royal Moerheim Nursery in Dedemsvaart, Overijssel), now a national trust property.[5]

In Germany during the 1930s and 'Forties, landscape architects worked to integrate the new autobahn system of high speed roads with rural environments. Chief adviser Alwin Seifert successfully advocated native planting and naturalistic design. German residential design was also moving in a more natural direction, away from traditional villa gardens with symmetrical, clipped evergreens and bedding plants.

Of course, this manicured style continues to dominate American gardens, making Karl Foerster's work newly relevant. He was the first to realize how ornamental grasses could give a garden structure and interest in the fall and winter, the off-seasons of other plants. Without grasses, the "natural" garden scheme with all-seasons interest could not make much sense. To make it work, Foerster selected wild grasses with garden characteristics—they wouldn't run rampant and turn the garden into a weed patch. He said, "Gras ist das Haar der Mutter Erde" (Grass is the hair of Mother Earth).[6] Seeing the way he used grasses in his classic volume, *Einzug der Gräser und Färne in die Garten—*

In the Netherlands, Mien Ruys creates a feeling of depth in a small garden with layers of plants, contrasting in foliage, size and color.
The beauty is in the proportions of the architectural framework—especially the paving which, as it moves through the garden, is softened and broken up by planting. The Dutch typically place paving brick on its narrow edge to give the illusion of greater space.
Photograph by James van Sweden.

repeated in separate locations, used as focal points or to screen—is to learn good design principles.

Many American designers share the vision of naturalism. Darrel Morrison, as an educator and champion of our native landscape, has been influential since the 1960s when his prairie restorations began to renew the aesthetic and ecological appeal of grasses. And, of course, Arthur Edward Bye, who stunned everyone in the 'Fifties with a plan of ultimate simplicity for a garden on the Atlantic shore, must be counted as a poetic presence in design.

THE EPHEMERAL

"Grasses dance in the breeze and are silent in the storm."

—*Arab Proverb*

Flower gardening is an art of time, like music and dance. At any season you see only part of nature's symphony, just one movement; even from day to day, you never know exactly how the garden is going to look. For instance, a pool with floating leaves is a wonderful surprise. Designers often do not think of that, but there are so many amazing dimensions to landscape design and living with designs over time. Design sets down the basic forms, but soon the garden is in nature's grip. Then, with careful nurturing, the garden's performance will outshine your imagination.

Beauty in gardens does not have to do with control or tidiness. Drifting cherry petals, seedheads bleaching out, a teak bench's patina, ice forming on a lily pool—such evidence of time's passage makes a garden beautiful. Because Japanese culture is highly attuned to ephemera, from the flutter of a leaf to Tokyo's thrilling chaos, their gardens are dominated by rigid forms which set off subtle changes. In the United States, lacking structure in the face of all-consuming progress, Americans have become blind to natural change unless it speaks boldly. Although every garden changes to some extent, our garden designs are more dramatically programmed than most to explode with change.

Above: Miscanthus sinensis in its native habitat—a mountainside on the island of Honshu, Japan. When using an international palette of plants, it is important to see and understand how a plant relates to its original landscape and associated plants. Photograph by James van Sweden.

Preceding page: The high drama of contemporary British naturalism is characteristic of Beth Chatto's Unusual Plants Nursery in central England. Here, a massive bog planting deals with the entire plane as a total picture. Chatto is inventive at combining textures, colors and sizes to paint the garden plane. Photograph by James van Sweden.

An early morning scene contrasts modern
Japan with the garden architecture and life of the
Edo Period (1603-1867) in Ritsurin Park in the town
of Takamatsu, on the island of Shikoku.
Feudal lords and courtesans once played a game by the
stream which flows through this pavilion. The object
was to compose a poem before a cup of
sake floated by. The penalty was to drink the contents.
Photograph by James van Sweden.

ROMANCE

The art of enchantment is at the heart of informal garden
design. Its potions are concealment, mystery, enticement,
intrigue and discovery. Garden structure throughout history has plied this art in a myriad of ways. Like learning to
write by reading good books, you can learn about designing
space through experiencing great gardens.

Hamburg's Planten un Blomen is full of lessons in
surprise. There are many intricate and interconnecting
spaces that never seem the same from visit to visit. This is
the design of mystery that pulls you through the garden.
The Japanese do this in even the smallest of spaces. They
will erect a piece of fence with a gate, like a smokescreen,
just to fool the eye and add yet another layer of penetration.
In the same way, we try to place sculpture as a divider to
entice and provide direction. A pathway also encourages
exploration when laid out in a "dogleg" to conceal the
route. Sometimes romance is purely visual, as in the "dry
stream" illusion, where an irregular line of rocks piques
the imagination and leads the eye deeper into the garden.

Right: At the Temple Garden of Ryoan-ji, in Kyoto, Japan, the dripline border between the wooden temple floor and the gravel garden plane is a beautiful composition of polished basalt, rough-hewn granite blocks, smooth river rocks, and narrow granite which edges the raked gravel. Photograph by James van Sweden.

Opposite: Detail. "Four Balls," by Grace Knowlton, in the van Sweden Garden. Photograph by John Neubauer.

The seductive use of materials is everywhere in Japan. The closer you look, the more there is to see. Edges are often treated with a variety of materials; paths "erode" as they move into the garden, spaced farther and farther apart to slow progress and to refocus your attention on the nuances of another world in nature. In our designs, edges are also a unifying way to detail the meeting of soft garden and hard architecture. Stepping a terrace back and forth creates an undulating edge where, over time, planted alcoves will obscure straight lines and angles.

At Japan's famed Zen garden, Ryoan-ji, seeing how the wooden temple building meets the ground was a strong influence. Several layers interpose between the vertical wood structure and raked sand—large scale gravel, granite and black basalt—to make a transition that frames the garden. It is so important to take enough time to consider how to make a building meet the ground, and to make materials and finishes consistent throughout the executed garden.

TRANSFORMATION

> "I look at that big ball by Grace Knowlton and I always think of the moon."
>
> —J.v.S.

If the garden's first act is to entice through mystery and detail, its second act is to reward your involvement with personal discovery. The gardens of Kyoto teach us how to contemplate the meaning of every element, especially the

Comfortable chairs are drawn into niches along one of Planten un Blomen's perennial plantings. Flexible seating is desirable because it gives people a feeling of personal freedom within a public space. Photograph by Wolfgang Oehme.

way things are placed in space. In the dimension of time, equal value is accorded to the changes from season to season and moment to moment, from lichen encrustations to hourly shadows. In the cultural dimension, the stones stand in for other fabled images, such as animals or mountains. Still, you can appreciate Japanese gardens on a purely physical level, which is only enhanced by knowing the allusions.

Generally we do not see our garden designs in narrative or textual terms. When meanings come, it is more like standing on a shoreline and setting your mind loose to range across the sea. Out of vast, unknowable nature comes the freedom to form new thoughts, or to notice some tiny wonder as for the first time. But you could also look at a stone and see a turtle, like seeing shapes in clouds. It is not necessary that meaning be written in the garden, only that you discover personal meaning and be transformed.

We return again and again to Planten un Blomen's dramatic, flowing spaces and innovative planting designs. This fascinating public park (1,170 acres) in Hamburg, Germany, was designed by Karl Plomin in 1953 and has continued to evolve under the administration of the city parks department. Photograph, 1989, by Wolfgang Oehme.

BOLD SCALE

"I like to work with music when designing, especially Beethoven, Bach and Wagner. Sometimes I draw with huge gestures like a conductor. I don't hold back with music—I let it all flow."
                                                           —W.O.

Drama is a key aspect of our work. Since childhood, we both have been drawn to the theater, dance and music, where the bold lines of story, movement and melody inspire and enlarge the imagination. Design, too, must focus on excitement. Sadly, many people prefer to tame nature, when nature is truly wild.

Seeing the gardens of the English landscape school, especially those of Lancelot (Capability) Brown (1716–83), is to see drama designed on the grand scale. That stunning, bold line revolutionized spatial design throughout Europe and the Americas. One who was greatly influenced was Brasilian Roberto Burle Marx (b.1909), who studied in Germany and in turn has affected our work. Burle Marx

The Ministry of Defense in Brasilia, Brasil, designed by Roberto Burle Marx in 1970, is a relaxed landscape on a monumental scale. Yellow-flowered *Cassia* species (left) and *Mauritia vinifera* (buriti) are used as sculptural elements rising from masses of *Eragrostis curvula* (love grass) which blurs the pavement edge and complements the plane of water in the background. Photograph by James van Sweden.

was inspired by the Berlin botanic garden and by Karl Foerster's advocacy of designing for natural association. A plant collector from age seven, Burle Marx has said, "Plants are the chief actors in the gardens that I try to create." Plants are also part of his social agenda: "We [landscape designers] need to understand the problems of today's cities because gardens are not only to be seen, but to be lived in."[7] He told us, "We can invent a fantastic world . . . Being old, I am curious about each new thing I see. . . . How can I use this like a new color in painting? . . . . Each new plant teaches me something and enables me to express something about myself. . . . Plants begin to have meaning when used in large masses, like the English herbaceous border."[8] Always, he links the garden to unworked nature through abstract design and the use of native plants. Seeing his fabulous design at Monteiro Garden, Petropolis, Brasil, was an affirmation of all that we seek to do.

In England, both Regent's Park and Kew Gardens boast borders at a sweeping, immense scale. It is marvelous to see plants used in such rich combinations of color, confirming that the flower belongs in the public park. While these extremely complex borders are beautiful in their own way, they demand a great deal of maintenance.

The "California Style" was evolved by Thomas Church (1902–78) in response to small spaces and the modern family's need for low maintenance. His vocabulary of seatwalls, raised beds, asymmetrical plans and wood decks has been tremendously influential on modern garden design. Seeing how he used diagonal lines to expand the sense of space in the Sullivan Garden (1935, San Francisco) clearly inspired our solution to the Schneiderman Garden.

How stirring is the Japanese appreciation of scale. Their lily ponds are as large as possible in proportion to the space, much bigger than we ever would have designed before visiting Japan and seeing how they work. It is important that a water feature not look like a curious little detail within the design, like a dish garden on the table. A pond of significant size becomes a dramatic element that actually creates space—ambiguous space, because it gives no sense of its own scale. In this way, water can fool the eye, set off plantings and rocks, and seem to enlarge the garden.

The garden of Shugaku-in Imperial Villa in Kyoto, begun c. 1655, is the culmination of everything that inspires us in Japanese design. It contains the tremendous scale of a mountain landscape, borrowed with the "shakkei" technique, in which external views are integral to the design. This view of mountains and an enormous body of water is juxtaposed with small, wonderful details of buildings, fences, stone paths. Here is a full range of personal experience from intimate space to the whole world. Once space unfolds forever before you, it changes your life and the way you perceive.

MAINTENANCE IN AMERICA

Our work is simpler than design in Germany and Japan. Japanese gardens are attended daily to preserve their sculptural forms, even to the point of plucking pine needles by hand. The more complicated, busy German gardens are equally difficult, demanding minute-by-minute care. Indeed, intensive maintenance is a proud tradition. German landscape drawings are a tapestry of symbols for plants used in two's and three's. Mass quantities of annuals are used, requiring intensive removal of faded flowers and yearly replacement.

America, quite to the contrary, has no such tradition of maintenance. Intricate gardens would be destroyed by untrained, inexperienced crews. Weeds grow quickly and aggressively. In response to these conditions, we have gradually simplified and refined our design approach. With every garden, we learn. When we finally visited Germany together in 1981, we suddenly understood how strongly our work departs from its German antecedent.

We use hardy perennials in mass quantities because they hold up to winter frost and damp, and flower year after year. Herbaceous plants die down in autumn and grow back in the spring, although some foliage persists through winter. In regions of the United States without the rest period of winter, such as Florida, the Desert Southwest and Southern California, hardy perennials may wear themselves out. Fortunately, every region has its own palette of plants with dormant periods brought on by a dry season, temperature or day length. These plants are vigorous and

reliable over time, and they can perform in ever-changing layers of space and seasonal effects.

Although the modern American way of life does not leave much time for maintenance, any garden landscape will simply disappear without it. If gardens are to take their place in public, designers must find ways to make care affordable. The most important guarantee of low maintenance is an automatic irrigation system which waters the garden regularly. As with a limited budget, the requirement for economical and easy maintenance can actually stimulate creativity. Realistic constraints greatly influence our thinking and are the key to success. As a result, easy care becomes a wonderful perquisite: it may surprise everybody, but you can have beauty and drama with the plus of low maintenance, which is eminently practical for America.

That is why the Federal Reserve Garden marked a significant milestone in our development. Designed for easy maintenance, it returns a garden ethic to the public landscape. It shows how gardens are possible for all the people who don't have the opportunity to enjoy gardens in private life. In the majority of private situations, simple designs with hardy perennials require much less involvement by the non-gardener. Yet such a client can feel that his or her garden is the world's greatest. Why? Because it has been designed for easy maintenance and maximum drama to give the greatest possible satisfaction and show.

A fish pond in perfect proportion to the garden greets the visitor to a private home in Tokyo, Japan. This is the view from the foyer of the house—a lively interface of the architecture of house and terrace on the right, contrasting with the soft landscape edge. Photograph by James van Sweden.

Part II

Practice

Common Issues

Every design accounts for the client's program of needs, but our real starting point is with personal, physical experience. Space is measured and modulated according to the human body. In fact, we use the term "eyelid" to describe arbors and other structures that cap the view, sometimes shutting out visual clutter, and at other times connecting important lines. If a landscape is to be seen from a moving vehicle, its design addresses the lower-level viewer and the speed of passage. Tiny gardens often have their greatest impact on people seated indoors, where an eye-level view is tantamount to immersion in the plant world.

People want sensual stimulation; they take pleasure in movement and arrival; and they love a garden best if it gives a sense of security and wholeness. Such is true of all gardens, that they may fill the imagination with richly affecting sight and sound. People like to touch, too, so tactile character and contrast is a central proposition of our design, even more important than color.

A bold, sweeping line expands and connects the garden to the larger world. By the same token, intricate detail ensures that the closer you look at something, the more complex and interesting that little bit of the world becomes, ultimately enlarging the sense of space. Mixing the strategies of boldness and romance pulls the garden together, with the assistance of repeated plants and details. This principle of enlarging contrast is standard in our designs, no matter what the circumstance or client.

A world apart is the feeling everyone desires at the heart of the garden: it requires the qualities of completeness and distinction. We approach it by combining the designer's concern for structure with the gardener's delight in the seasonal dynamics of plants. The design works through unfolding layers of space and time.

From the entrance court at the Shockey Garden, cascading water makes a transition to the terrace 21 feet below. A meandering stairway alongside is softened here by *Astilbe* species (false spirea). Photograph by Michael McKinley.

Preceding page: The Shockey Garden in summer. Photograph by Michael McKinley.

LAYERS OF SPACE

A person is enticed to the garden by promising glimpses across layers of sun and shade. Once entered, the garden is a continuous discovery as the layers peel away and overlap, becoming interlocking volumes of planted and open spaces. The garden is designed in the round, so that it continues to make sense in every direction as you move through the unfolding spaces. Always, this "surround" provides a protective feeling and outward views. It is disappointing to see the garden all at once. A garden that surprises and allows for discovery is endlessly entertaining.

We organize every garden as a progression of spaces that become less geometric, more irregular as they move out from a building. Function comes first in the design process because it is more useful to ask how an area should work, than what it should be. That is why garden areas are often located in relation to living activities within the house: a breakfast terrace is near the dining room, and a service area near the kitchen. Outdoor spaces, however, are more complex to design than the common notion of the "outdoor room" might suggest. Architects know that the foundation of a house, no matter what its actual dimensions, is dwarfed by the ground plane and the sky. Only when the verticals are erected and the roof beams added does the enclosed space enlarge visually. Proportion is the key to structuring outdoor space, and it is especially important in the small garden, where enlargement is the designer's first task.

Because a garden can rarely be enlarged in actual square feet, extension must take place in the imagination, through vertical layering or contrasts of scale. Spatial modulation can be handled much as art gallery expositions are designed, where you walk around panels that divide the space. In addition to subdividing the space into layers with design elements such as terraces, stairs, trees, large grasses and sculpture, different levels for specific uses enlarge the garden functionally. Space is perceived as more complicated and more interesting than it would be if left undeveloped. Oversized specimens, such as *Hibiscus moscheutos* or *Miscanthus floridulus,* can give importance to a restricted, insignificant area. There is nothing more diminishing than the precious effect of tiny plants in tiny gardens.

Design "events" also help to expand limited spaces by creating interest, especially in neglected "back alley" areas. At the Slifka Garden on Long Island, a secondary gate accents a far corner where stepping stones curve around to the basement rooms that service the pool. Another scheme could have been more direct, but why treat utilitarian areas like second-class citizens when they can add so much?

Opposite: A bold line of *Rudbeckia fulgida* 'Goldsturm' undulates along the ground plane, seemingly into infinity. This layered, late summer view of the Federal Reserve Gardens starts at a sculpture by Raya Bodnarchuk, standing against the feathery inflorescence of *Calamagrostis acutiflora stricta,* with the creamy-lime blooms of *Sophora japonica* (Japanese pagoda tree) overhead. Photograph by James van Sweden.

Pools and lawns, along with paved terraces, provide open spaces in contrast to layered volumes of plants. Lawn, however, is not a given in these gardens. Its long-term costs—consuming energy for mowing, watering and chemical treatment—are difficult to justify, so we require that any lawn address a specific purpose and scale it to suit that role. Some legitimate uses might include entertainment, sunbathing or children's play. We advise clients to think of the lawn as just one part of the overall garden, and to retain only as much as needed. Like lawn, water is a high-maintenance inclusion, but it is well worth the upkeep. Water provides a sleek, reflective surface, a fascinating source of sound and movement, and sometimes recreation. When contrasted with intricate plantings, the simplicity of lawn and water can fool the eye into perceiving an enlarged sense of scale.

Always, our goal is to design the garden as an enveloping composition that uses the entire visual and physical space available to it. We think of it as theater in the round. A total garden integrates all its uses and elements into a single design of plants, paving and water, with spaces for working, relaxing and entertaining. The house is a pavilion within this interlocking garden sculpture, especially when a terrace is on grade with the ground floor of the house. Where land is very flat, we use soil (often excavated from pools) to create mounds toward the outer reaches of the garden. Lifting the garden's edge creates depth, enclosure and culmination in the distance.

As an extension of the house, the garden is a series of spaces designed to suit living patterns. In the Draper Garden, a large "living room" spins around a *Cornus kousa*; a broad flight of steps descends from the antechamber where guests are received into the garden. Wooden stairs lead up to the French doors to the living room. Photograph by John Neubauer.

IN TIME

The one constant of every garden is change, and perennials are ideally suited to express it. When perennials constitute most of a planting plan, seasonal variations can be designed to welcome the rush of spring growth, accommodate the lushness of summer, and overcome the all-too-common aversion to winter's spare landscape. Seasons radically change the spatial layers, adding to the ongoing drama.

In the nakedness of late winter, spring awakens the earth. At first a few bulbs emerge and then the tempo begins to accelerate: ferns are unfurling, later bulbs are pushing up and perennials are turning green and starting to grow again. What began in the stillness of winter has become a time of great movement, of rumblings in the earth and of immense change.

As the year unfolds, the space gradually fills up. Walls and external clutter disappear. When the garden's growth is nigh to bursting, the grasses thick and flowers profuse, it is summer. Here is a new landscape of full-blown scale and lazy tempo. Colors ripen in autumn as, almost imperceptibly, the plants begin to dry.

At first frost, the garden's image suddenly reverses, like a photographic negative in which dark evergreens stand forth in elegant, formal contrast to pale, gilded grasses. In proportion, deciduous plants comprise about two-thirds of the garden, balanced against one-third evergreens. Seedheads are beads of sienna and ebony; textures are sere and rustling. Winter's dry bouquet is a reservoir of distilled sunlight in suspended growth until the cycle begins again. As spring approaches and the herbaceous material is cut down, the absolutely clean, mulched space is very refreshing. That is when sculptural forms speak out to "hold" visual space.

The garden is a continuous stream of moments, acutely temporal, that quicken the senses and romance the observer. Subtle changes occur in the course of a single day; from week to week, changes are more marked. Something is always happening. The end product is dynamic movement from one season to the next and immense variation in scale, color and volume throughout the year.

With the elements of surprise and humor, the garden becomes a character in its own right. In the Rosenberg Garden on Long Island, for instance, the quality of light is like an expression that flickers across a person's face. In the morning and evening, the grasses are backlit, and all the while wind is shuffling the leaves and setting the seedheads to nodding. The landscape is a kinetic sculpture to be seen in four dimensions, including time.

RECLAIMING THE PUBLIC REALM

American cities and towns exist in nature, but largely ignore or suppress it to the great expense of human health, safety and welfare. Gardens can be a powerful tool of efforts to reclaim the urban wasteland and make it hospitable to life. Nature's unfolding drama belongs to all people, especially those without access to home gardening. When people go outside to have lunch, relax, or meet a friend, they need comfortable places to sit. They like to feel surrounded by a loose screen of plants, protected and not endangered. Whether public or private, the principles of spatial layering and temporal change are what makes a garden a garden. These principles create a human scale that mediates between nature and the city. Intimacy with nature belongs in the city, so that people may find a congenial niche in which to anchor themselves amid the hustle and bustle.

A modest node in the plan of Washington, D.C., the German-American Friendship Garden refreshes the visitor with fountains, delights the eye with color, and offers comfortable benches on which to rest. Photograph by Michael McKinley.

The public garden is on stage every day of the year and must be designed to attract passers-by, both on foot and in cars. In the hurried city, bolder design is "readable" at higher speeds and greater distances. To catch the eye, an undulating line of planting may sweep to the edge of the street, then dive deep into the garden space. Just as the garden must be dramatic when passed at 35 miles per hour, it should also be as beautiful as a two-dimensional painting when seen from tall buildings nearby. Generally, planting plans are simplified in these situations, using a smaller plant list in larger blocks of space for clarity and contrast.

A corner lot, the Anne Lloyd Garden's
woodland landscape has been reclaimed from the street.
At the bottom of the garden, a terrace overlooks
the ponds created by damming the stream;
four steps lead down into the water. This was the
setting used for "Silver Tree,"
as photographed for the catalogue,
"Lila Katzen: Sculpture Returns to the Garden."
The 1982 exhibition was landscaped by
Oehme, van Sweden and Associates in the Alex
Rosenberg Gallery, New York City.
Photograph by Gretchen Tatje.

Overleaf: The distinction between inside
and out blurs in the Sheffield Garden, Washington, D.C.
Like stained glass, *Parthenocissus quinquefolia*
(Virginia creeper) frames the garden view from the
living room. The fountain is on axis with
the front door; urns are placed diagonally on the
coping, layering and giving depth to the
scene. Simplicity of planting design enlarges the scale:
Pennisetum alopecuroides acts like a balustrade
atop a retaining wall, and *Miscanthus
sinensis gracillimus* gives a delicate "hedge"
effect along the lily pool's right side.
Photograph by Bradley Olman.

RESCUING THE PRIVATE GARDEN

In the 'Teens and 'Twenties, the automobile was virtually worshipped for its liberating and powerful qualities. Now nearly every front yard in America belongs to the street, and we often find a garage where the garden should be. Perhaps we hate the car because our parents loved it so much, although it is ultimately a philosophical point that one should have as much space as possible to enjoy the outdoors. We are determined to put the car in its place.

The front garden has the considerable task of separating the public street from private space, while presenting a neighborly face to the world. Traditionally, people have given up and simply planted a stock mixture of evergreens along the foundations of the house. We utterly reject foundation planting as waste. Instead of the "front yard" starting at the facade of the house, we move the line of demarcation closer to the street, placing trees and shrubs well away from the house to divide the private from the public domain. Pulling the plants away from the foundations comfortably mediates between home and street to open up a new zone for family living.

Just as the old-fashioned front lawn gave itself away to the street, so did the side and back yard give valuable space over to the driveway and garage. We try to put the car as close to the street as possible. In this way, millions of American homeowners can rescue a big piece of their backyards. Removing a real estate "asset" can be a tough decision, until you imagine a car going right through the garden. What a sore thumb!

Attitude is an important aspect of rescuing the private garden from conformity. At first, garden newcomers may say, "I don't really want anything that's too different from my neighbors." We ask, "Do you want us to design down to your neighbors?" Of course their response is, "No." Ultimately, a garden is a personal expression of nature. Our clients are not conformists—they are daring and willing to go out on a limb.

An Anthology of Private
and Public Gardens

A GARDENER'S GARDEN

The Vollmer Garden

A wash in a suburban sea of lawn, the traditional house was anchored with typical foundation plantings. But the Vollmers were anything but typical. They were willing to challenge the status quo, approve unfamiliar plants, and take on the garden as an evolving creature. Pauline Vollmer belonged to a garden club and cultivated roses; Leo Vollmer liked golden orfe—an ornamental fish from Germany. Both were disappointed with the previous efforts of local nurseries. Our subsequent design work has been incremental, reflecting change in the Vollmers' lives over the decades and gradually supplanting the lawns.

First, we regrouped the foundation shrub plantings as the basis for a screen between the street and the dining room window. The asymmetrical layer of plants interposed between public and private space is our basic principle of front yard design. Originally, some lawn was kept on both sides of the existing curved walkway to tie into neighboring lawn. Eventually, the Vollmers tired of mowing and asked us to remove the remaining lawn in favor of perennials.

The private garden behind the house is a series of three terraces stepping down an easy slope, connected by stepping stones through planting beds. Seated on the pre-existing upper terrace next to the house, the view takes in many layers, beginning with a foreground of *Pinus mugo* (Swiss mountain pine), a variety of ornamental grasses and the elegant, multi-trunked form of a *Carpinus caroliniana* (American hornbeam) at the terrace edge.

The front yard is no longer a public space when it is treated as a textured ground plane from which sculptural elements rise to shield views from the street. *Opposite:* Next to the front door, a specimen *Ilex pedunculosa* screens the dining room from the walkway; the finely-textured *Fargesia nitida* seems to soften the right corner of the house. *Above:* Diners enjoy a view into their own private garden room, without exposure to passers-by. The yellow spires of *Lysimachia punctata* (garden loosestrife) light up the lush setting. Photographs by Michael McKinley.

The lay of the land has a great effect on the way a design develops. As the slope moves down from the house, the garden appears remote. Planted layers of space, however, will create mystery and draw the eye into lower areas. Stepping out onto Pauline Vollmer's living room terrace, the view into the garden's depth seems limitless. Fences and neighboring houses are virtually invisible. Photograph by Michael McKinley.

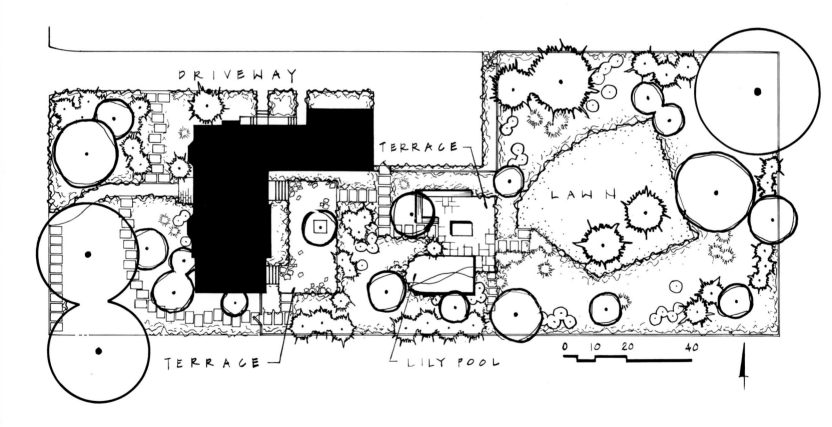

DRIVEWAY

TERRACE

LAWN

TERRACE

LILY POOL

0   10   20   40

Holding the edge of a terrace against a
higher slope, a seatwall is secluded behind a tracery of
Calamagrostis acutiflora stricta in the foreground.
Macleaya cordata just behind the bench
is surrounded with *Rudbeckia fulgida* 'Goldsturm',
the bright spots of yellow echoed by the
dazzling variegated foliage of *Miscanthus sinensis
strictus* at the far end. Photograph by
Michael McKinley.

A walk should encounter obstacles and
be its own space within the garden. From the living
room terrace, stepping stones meander down
to the lower terrace and lily pool, situated in the
middle third of the garden space. The garden builds up
visual power as your eye moves past the large
Maackia amurensis (maackia) at the entrance of the
terrace to sunlit plantings in the background. On
the table, "Crow," cast aluminum, by Lonnie
Joe Edwards. Photograph by Michael McKinley.

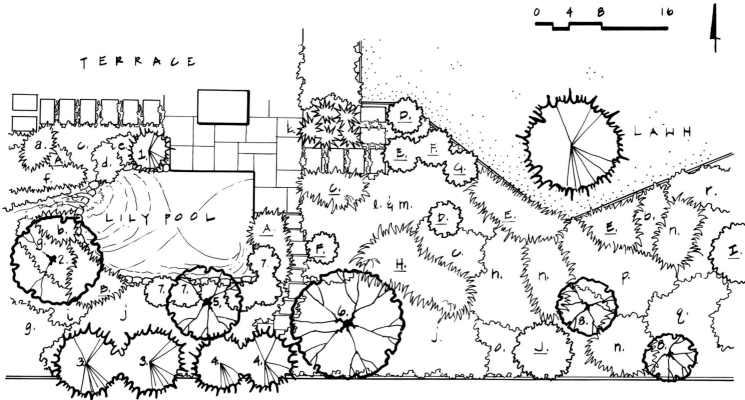

PERENNIALS

a. *Bergenia cordifolia*

b. *Iris sibirica*   (Siberian iris)

c. *Corydalis lutea*   (yellow corydalis)

d. *Lobelia cardinalis*   (cardinal flower)

e. *Euonymus fortunei*   (spreading euonymus)

f. *Polygonum cuspidatum compactum*   (Japanese knotweed)

g. *Epimedium* x *versicolor*   (long-spur epimedium)

h. *Brunnera macrophylla*

i. *Hosta sieboldiana*

j. *Macleaya cordata*

k. *Yucca filamentosa*

l. *Erica carnea*   (spring heather)

m. *Calluna vulgaris*   (Scotch heather)

n. *Hemerocallis* sp.   (daylily)

o. *Monarda* sp.   (bee balm)

p. *Lythrum salicaria* 'Morden's Pink'

q. *Hibiscus moscheutos*

r. *Ceratostigma plumbaginoides*

s. *Sedum* x *telephium* 'Autumn Joy'

t. *S. spurium* 'Album Superbum'   (evergreen stonecrop)

u. *Polygonum affine*   (Himalayan fleeceflower)

v. *Pontederia cordata*   (pickerelweed)

w. *Calluna* sp.   (heather)

GRASSES & SEDGES

A. *Carex muskingumensis*   (palm sedge)

B. *C. pendula*

C. *Festuca* sp.   (fescue)

D. *Spodiopogon sibiricus*

E. *Panicum virgatum* 'Haense Herms'

F. *Molinia arundinacea* 'Windspiel'   (tall purple moor grass)

G. *Miscanthus sinensis purpurascens*

H. *Pennisetum alopecuroides*

I. *Miscanthus floridulus*

J. *M. sinensis condensatus*   (purple-blooming Japanese silver grass)

K. *Pennisetum orientale*   (orient fountain grass)

TREES & SHRUBS

1. *Pinus peuce*   (Macedonian pine)

2. *Carpinus caroliniana*   (American hornbeam)

3. *Tsuga canadensis*   (Canadian hemlock)

4. *Taxus* x *media hicksii*   (Anglo-Japanese yew)

5. *Salix purpurea nana*   (dwarf basket willow)

6. *Pinus thunbergiana*   (Japanese black pine)

7. *Lonicera pileata*   (privet honeysuckle)

8. *Rhus typhina laciniata*   (staghorn sumac)

9. *Pinus mugo*   (Swiss mountain pine)

10. *Maackia amurensis*   (amur maackia)

*Common names are provided in parentheses for plants that are not listed in the "Glossary of Favorite Plants," page 271. When an initial is given for the genus in the botanical name, as in "C. pendula," it refers to the genus preceding it in the list, eg. "Carex muskingumensis." Abbreviations include: "sp." for "species," and "x" for "hybrid."

Right: Set into one side of the terrace, the lily pool offers a striking contrast between a sharp, paved edge and a soft, naturalistic edge. The red-flowering, native *Lobelia cardinalis* (cardinal flower) in the foreground characterizes the transitional marsh plantings between water and high ground. Photograph by Henry Groskinsky.

Opposite: Stepping stones from pond terrace through the meadow-like border to the lawn beyond. The strong forms of *Yucca filamentosa* establish a gateway from the lower terrace through a meadow-like border featuring the soft textures of *Calluna vulgaris* (heather). Photograph by Michael McKinley.

"This garden is an environment of serenity, with a fascinating variety of forms and textures."
—Pauline E. Vollmer

Through the branching traceries are inviting glimpses of the lower terrace, designed to meet Leo Vollmer's request for a fish pond. We situated the pond to one side, a third of the way toward the back property line. Sharp-edged bluestone coping cantilevers over the water in total contrast to the far side, a soft verge of pebbles and plantings. In and around the pool, the plants are layered according to cultural conditions; they progress from water lilies to marsh plants, such as *Iris sibirica* (Siberian iris) and *Lobelia cardinalis* (cardinal flower) to dry uplanders like *Epimedium* x *versicolor* 'Sulphureum' and various *Hosta* species.

Seated on the pool terrace in the garden's early years, you could hardly see the lawn that was originally tailored as an additional terrace for big parties. Its angular shape gave the lawn visual perspective and movement, while three pines planted in the middle of the space kept the whole area from being seen at once. The property line was screened by existing evergreens, to which *Pinus thunbergiana* (Japanese black pine) and *Tsuga canadensis* (Canadian hemlock) were added for density. Inevitably the Vollmers' garden grew along with their taste for plants. Just as it happened with the front yard, the rear lawn terrace gradually was overtaken by a host of new plants, featuring the textures of *Calluna vulgaris* (Scotch heather).

Placing higher plants toward the street makes it possible to have a lavish garden between the curb and the house, reclaiming the front yard for the people who live there. In this case, it is the "New American Garden," designed as a prototype for a public education center at the United States National Arboretum in Washington, D.C. The garden's role is to welcome and to entertain, just as any sociable homeowner would want, except the terrace is larger and more ceremonial.

Beyond the vivid foreground of *Imperata cylindrica* 'Red Baron' (Japanese blood grass), a sculpture by John Cavanaugh, "Demeter," faces toward the house to define the garden's orientation and to hold the terrace edge in winter. This garden is so dramatic that it diverts attention from the ordinary ranch-style structure, which once was a real home. Photograph by Michael McKinley.

In winter, the garden spins gold against the chocolate brown of *Rudbeckia fulgida* 'Goldsturm'. There is a careful balance of deciduous and evergreen plants, playing up the ravishing borrowed scenery of the National Arboretum. Photograph by James van Sweden.

Mini-meadows reclaim two tiny front yards in Washington, D.C. Plants cascade over walks and soften all the hard edges, bringing the houses down to the ground plane with the dramatic, showy effects possible in sunny southern exposures. The smaller the space, the more carefully you have to choose among plants for texture.

The Mary Evans garden (left) is a pastiche of sunny meadow plants, including *Ceratostigma plumbaginoides, Pennisetum alopecuroides, Yucca filamentosa,* and *Rudbeckia fulgida* 'Goldsturm'. Two trees—on the right, a *Hamamelis mollis* 'Brevipetala' (Chinese witch hazel) and on the left, an *Amelanchier canadensis*—give privacy from the street, only about 18 feet from the attractively renovated front door. Photograph by James van Sweden.

In the Littlefields' third garden of Oehme and van Sweden design (opposite), the border is a collection of sun-loving plants. *Sedum* x *telephium* 'Autumn Joy' complements the red brick walk, which is shielded from the driveway at left by *Ilex* x *attenuata* 'Fosteri'. The traceries of *Molinia arundinacea* 'Windspiel' form a "gateway" near the front door, with *Pennisetum alopecuroides* on the left and *Miscanthus sinensis purpurascens* on the right. It doesn't matter that the house is tiny or close to the street when you can endow a relatively small space with a big bang. Photograph by Volkmar Wentzel.

NATURE FILLS AN URBAN SPACE

The van Sweden Garden

In spring, when ornamental grasses are cut down and the *Miscanthus floridulus* is merely a brush, the garden's limits are clear. Grace Knowlton's sculpture speaks and the "dry stream" of stepping stones is fully revealed. From the vantage of the kitchen table, the view through open French doors takes in the 800 spring bulbs that are planted every year. Photographs by John Neubauer.

The single most important thing we found about this Georgetown garden was its gentle slope up toward the back. Only 17 x 55 feet, the theatrical quality of its "raked stage" provided the basis for mystery and visual depth. We opened up the back of the house with French doors so that the kitchen would flow into the garden. Just outside is a very narrow terrace, only seven feet deep. Planting seems to come right up to the house, virtually at eye level from the kitchen table.

Layers begin in the foreground, as you look through and around a delicate *Magnolia virginiana* positioned atop the retaining wall. Steps mount from the left to a landing from which stepping stones lead diagonally toward a *Miscanthus floridulus* placed against the stockade fence, then turn back toward another *M. floridulus* at the center. The meandering line and vertical plant accents work together to lead the eye deeper into a scene which is not completely revealed, even in so tiny a space. Designed as a "dry stream," the stone path emphasizes the gentle incline, showing up most clearly in the spring.

This modest garden changes character continuously with the seasons. In late winter, Grace Knowlton's sculpture, "Four Balls," takes over visually. These spheres are infinitely flexible. It is fun to play with their positions, but they also have a life of their own, creeping imperceptibly down the slope over weeks and months.

In addition to the sculpture, the *Hamamelis mollis* (Chinese witch hazel), *Salix caprea* (pussy willow), *Mahonia bealei,* and *Carex morrowii variegata* hold the view when everything else is cut down in early March. The immense *Ailanthus altissima* (tree-of-heaven) draped in mature *Hedera helix* (English ivy) is always present as a giant point of drama. Surely it was planted in the original garden, more than a century ago.

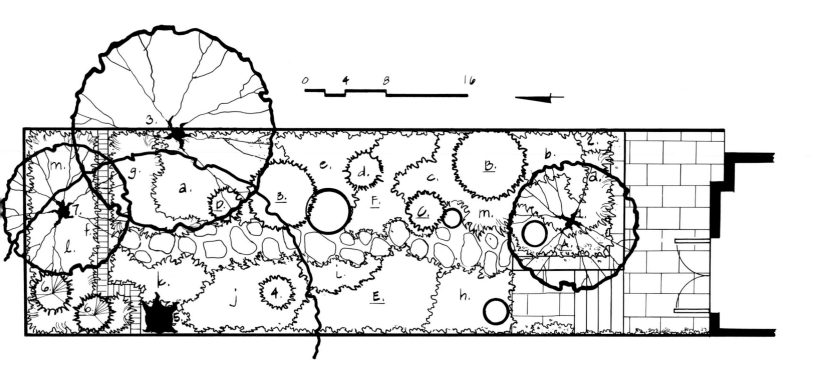

PERENNIALS

a. *Epimedium* x *versicolor* 'Sulphureum'

b. *Adiantum pedatum*   (maidenhair fern)

c. *Brunnera macrophylla*

d. *Hibiscus moscheutos*

e. *Perovskia atriplicifolia*

f. *Hosta sieboldiana*

g. *Ligularia dentata* 'Desdemona'

h. *Acanthus hungaricus*

i. *Rudbeckia fulgida* 'Goldsturm'

j. *Osmunda regalis*   (royal fern)

k. *Hosta plantaginea*   (fragrant plantain lily)

l. *Rodgersia pinnata*   (rodgersia)

m. *Liriope muscari* 'Big Blue'

GRASSES & SEDGES

A. *Carex morrowii variegata*

B. *Miscanthus floridulus*

C. *Pennisetum viridescens*

D. *Miscanthus sinensis gracillimus*

E. *Calamagrostis acutiflora stricta*

F. *Pennisetum alopecuroides*

TREES, SHRUBS & VINES

1. *Magnolia virginiana*

2. *Lonicera pileata*   (privet leaf honeysuckle)

3. *Salix* sp.   (pussy willow)

4. *Fargesia nitida*

5. *Ailanthus altissima*   (tree-of-heaven)

6. *Ilex* x *attenuata* 'Fosteri'

7. *Hamamelis mollis* 'Brevipetala'   (Chinese witch hazel)

8. *Hedera helix*   (English ivy)

9. *Jasminum nudiflorum*   (winter jasmine)

Mid-winter. Photograph
by John Neubauer.

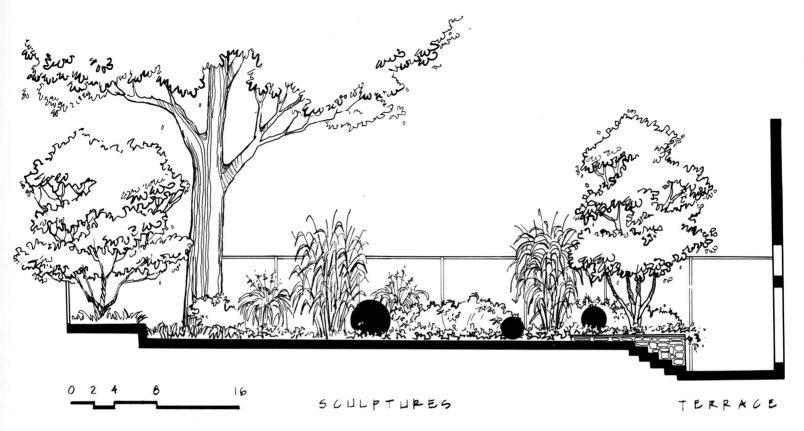

0 2 4   8   16

SCULPTURES   TERRACE

Right: By mid-summer, luxuriant growth transforms the space completely. *Calamagrostis acutiflora stricta* follows the line of stepping stones, now buried in the "meadow." When doors are opened wide the kitchen and small terrace at house level flow together as continuous space. Photograph by Michael McKinley.

Opposite: A multi-trunked *Magnolia virginiana* modulates the space between house and garden, providing scale and foreground to the view. In late spring, the tree is in full bloom with fragrant white flowers; their perfume drifts down onto the terrace at night. Pots are planted with *Lantana* cultivars for bright color, and the globes of *Allium giganteum* (ornamental onion) stand out against *Calamagrostis acutiflora stricta*, which is already coming into bloom along the path. Photograph by Valerie Brown.

COUNTRY LIVING IN TOWN

The Gelman Garden

This is a garden for grownups, kids and the explorer in everyone. The Gelmans wanted to develop their whole property as a garden from end to end. Specific requests included a swimming pool, a children's play area with lawn space, and a front yard in sympathy with the suburban neighborhood. A growing, active family needs lots of different spaces, so the plan began with circulation, as is often the case.

We deliberately designed the progression from formal to informal spaces down a dramatic hillside to capture the borrowed view of a perfectly maintained fairway of a neighboring country club. The front garden flanks an entry walk with plantings, and asymmetrically places a small lawn to one side, along a new fence and gate to the private garden. The bluestone coping along the edge of the lawn can double as a narrow walkway to the gate.

On the other side of the fence, irregularly-spaced stone pavers lead across plush lawn toward a new veranda off the back of the house. Taking the architect's cue in the country-style veranda, we selected a flooring of bluestone and carried it onto a paved terrace and into many details, such as edgings.

Throughout the garden, architecture plays against the "natural" scenery that is pulled into the garden's physical and visual domain. The dry-laid stone retaining wall which carves out the pool terrace makes a graceful curve toward the woods and the distant view. A simple border of plants at the far end of the pool does not compete with the view, while making the precipitous edge feel safer. It is a soft "balustrade" to be looked through—a layer that enlarges the garden by making the distance seem even farther away and more mysterious.

As you move downslope from the Gelman home toward the woodland stream, spaces become more and more natural. *Opposite:* The slope below the pool terrace is planted like a meadow, with *Pennisetum alopecuroides* and *Lobelia cardinalis* (red cardinal flower). (Photograph by Michael McKinley.) *Above:* Like a series of plateaus, terraces step down the hillside from the house to the pool and, finally, to the play lawn. Photograph by James van Sweden.

Mid-summer. Photograph by Michael McKinley.

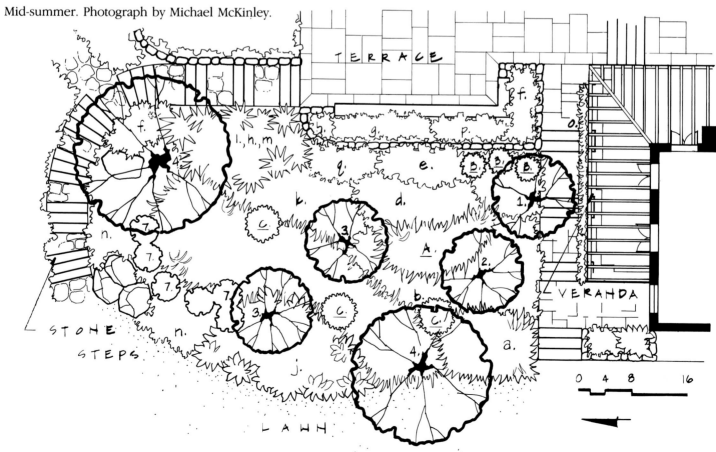

TERRACE

STONE

STEPS

VERANDA

LAWN

0   4   8   16

PERENNIALS

a. *Iris sibirica* (Siberian iris)

b. *Stokesia laevis* (Stokes' aster)

c. *Geranium macrorrhizum* 'Spessart' (hardy cranesbill)

d. *Sedum* x *telephium* 'Autumn Joy'

e. *Hibiscus moscheutos* 'Mixed Colors'

f. *Acanthus hungaricus*

g. *Coreopsis verticillata* 'Moonbeam'

h. *Perovskia atriplicifolia*

i. *Hemerocallis* sp. (daylily)

j. *Hosta* x 'Honeybells' (plantain lily)

k. *Aster* x *frikartii* 'Moench'

l. *Yucca filamentosa*

m. *Ceratostigma plumbaginoides*

n. *Bergenia cordifolia*

o. *Liriope muscari* 'Big Blue'

p. *Vinca major* (greater periwinkle)

q. *Lythrum salicaria* 'Morden's Pink'

r. *Lantana* sp. (shrub verbena)

s. *Rudbeckia fulgida* 'Goldsturm'

GRASSES & SEDGES

A. *Miscanthus sinensis purpurascens*

B. *Molinia arundinacea* 'Windspiel' (tall purple moor grass)

C. *Miscanthus sinensis gracillimus*

TREES & SHRUBS

1. *Oxydendrum arboreum* (sourwood)

2. *Cornus mas* (cornelian cherry)

3. *C. kousa*

4. *Zelkova serrata* 'Greenvase'

5. *Cornus florida* (flowering dogwood)

6. *Ilex* x *attenuata* 'Fosteri'

7. *Hydrangea paniculata* (panicle hydrangea)

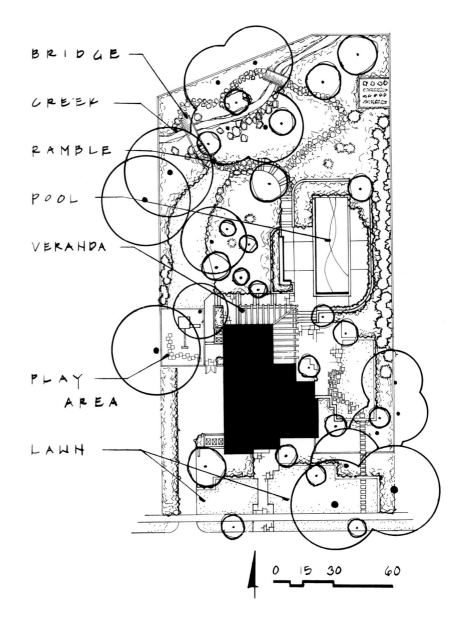

BRIDGE
CREEK
RAMBLE
POOL
VERANDA
PLAY AREA
LAWN

0 15 30 60

Above: From the main terrace, the
swimming pool is a mirror that reflects the sky
and trees which frame a "window" to
the borrowed scenery of a golf course beyond.
Photograph by James van Sweden.

Top right: A flexible design will allow the
playground to change as the Gelman children grow.
A woodchip surface over sand ensures soft
landings; the retaining wall of vertical railroad ties is
very popular for clambering. Right: A natural
stone path and steps lead up to the children's lawn
from the bridge. Photographs by Michael McKinley.

Opposite: The stream is edged with rock to control erosion during storms and give a sense of movement through the garden. Stepping stones to the right make a pleasant ramble between the bridges. Photograph by Volkmar Wentzel.

"Our garden is a place to enjoy being with children and friends. It is, in some ways, the most important 'room' in our house."
—Susan and Michael Gelman

Plantings flow around the pool and cascade down the hillside to the lower children's lawn. The original planting plan for this hillside included three *Cornus kousa* and created the kind of incident that so often improves a design. After the trees were planted, it turned out that they blocked the family's favorite new view from their dining spot on the veranda. Accordingly, we relocated the trees as a frame, and arranged the perennials by height to funnel the view. This adjusted planting design has made the slope a visual bridge to the woods.

The lower lawn is specifically tailored for throwing a ball or a frisbee. We designed a mulched playground to fit the children's play equipment; their father built the sandbox. Landscape timbers form a retaining wall that is fun to climb. The adventure continues in the lower garden, where an existing stream was once just a leftover space. Two wooden bridges, designed by the architect to echo the veranda's balustrade, cross the stream to a rambling trail on the opposite bank, and bring the entire property into the garden's scope.

STREET

WALK

TERRACE

POOL

0 4 8 16   32

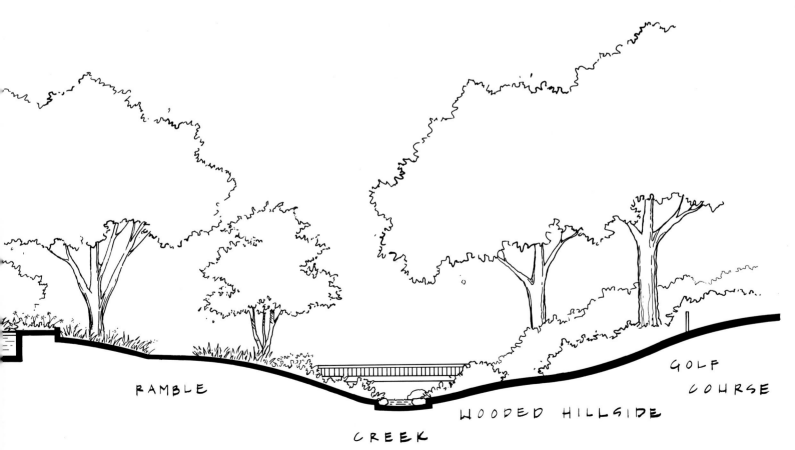

RAMBLE

CREEK

WOODED HILLSIDE

GOLF COURSE

The Board of Trustees at the University of Minnesota in St. Paul understood that their campus speaks about the institution's character, so they commissioned a new landscape plan and gardens to reflect the diversity and high caliber of the academic community. Hardy perennials were chosen to withstand U.S.D.A. Zone 4 conditions where winter temperatures can dip as low as 30 degrees below zero.

At one end of the central mall, the plaza in front of Johnston Hall attracts activity to a monumental space. Umbrella tables and such plantings as *Coreopsis verticillata* 'Moonbeam' introduce human scale and make a pleasant spot to sit in the shade. The Minneapolis skyline is just visible to the right of Johnston Hall.

Another garden, the Morrill Hall Plaza, is located on a diagonal pedestrian axis of the campus on top of the central parking garage. The Plaza is flanked on the left by the administration building (Morrill Hall) and, on the right, the Northrop Memorial Auditorium; in the center distance is Johnston Hall. Views such as this, where bright bands of *Calamagrostis acutiflora stricta* are reiterated by a far sweep of *Rudbeckia fulgida* 'Goldsturm', are working to enhance the public image and appeal of the University of Minnesota. Photographs by Michael McKinley.

HILLSIDE COLLAGE

A Suburban Residence

I t is one thing to locate a house, tennis court, pool and driveway upon a two-and-a-half-acre parcel; it is another to fit them into a sloping landscape. Grading was the key to this project. It dramatizes the entrance, diminishes the athletic club scale of the tennis court, and mediates between the house and the surrounding woods.

To screen the tennis court from view of the entry drive and the house, we placed it at a lower level, beyond planted berms. The bulk of stone retaining walls is softened by terraces overhung with pendulous plants. These walls "hold" the upper level and create a sense of security across the dramatically changing grade.

Mounding also places the house more comfortably at the crest of the driveway which slopes upward so sharply. A planting island is exaggerated in size to meet the topographic scale and graded as a convex surface. Its raised, dome-like form gives more height to the already sculptural planting and connects it with the overall garden to support the house. More than a simple driveway circle, the planting island is a kinetic landscape to which the driveway is quite subsidiary.

The swimming pool is built into the slope at a lower level than the main terrace level of the house, to be invisible in the winter. Its elliptical shape and black color evoke a reflecting pond in the woods. Two different paving surfaces hint at this cant: a stone terrace on the house side of the pool meets a wooden deck that projects into the trees. Linking the materials of architecture with the natural landscape can be especially important in a property closely framed by woods.

No one had ever seen anything like this landscape design locally, with absolutely no lawn, at such a scale. Perhaps it arouses the owners' love of prairie—obviously these are daring, brave clients.

This is a garden without lawn. A small grove of *Betula nigra* (river birch) screens the front door from the street. The driveway edge is softened by *Lysimachia clethroides* (gooseneck loosestrife on the left.). (Photograph by Michael McKinley.) *Above: Juniperus davurica expansa* (Parsons juniper) is backed with *Cytisus* x *praecox* (Warminster broom). *Miscanthus sinensis 'Malepartus'* trembles above pink spikes of *Liatris spicata*. Photograph by James van Sweden.

PERENNIALS

a. *Yucca filamentosa*

b. *Liriope muscari* 'Big Blue'

c. *Aster* x *frikartii* 'Moench'

d. *Coreopsis verticillata* 'Moonbeam'

e. *Acanthus hungaricus*

f. *Achillea filipendulina*

g. *Lythrum salicaria* 'Roberts'   (carmine red loosestrife)

h. *Caryopteris* x *clandonensis*   (bluebeard)

i. *Perovskia atriplicifolia*

j. *Liatris spicata*

GRASSES & SEDGES

A. *Spodiopogon sibiricus*

B. *Miscanthus sinensis gracillimus*

C. *Calamagrostis acutiflora stricta*

D. *Molinia arundinacea* 'Karl Foerster'   (tall purple moor grass)

TREES & SHRUBS

1. *Betula nigra*   (river birch)

2. *Cytisus* x *praecox* 'Moonlight'   (Warminster broom)

3. *Juniperus davurica expansa*   (Parsons juniper)

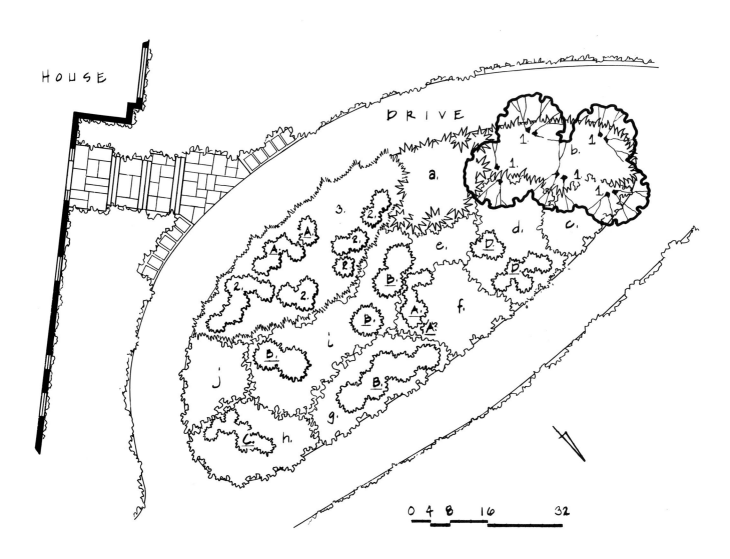

Mid-summer. Photograph by Michael McKinley.

Opposite: Planting along the swimming pool's edge softens it and casts reflections in the water—especially effective when the plants are lit at night. The pool's ultramarine color enhances its reflections and naturalism. A half-level down from the main floor of the house, the pool terrace is a secluded environment, out of view in winter. Rising from the slope below the deck is a *Miscanthus floridulus. Right:* Approaching the pool terrace from the tennis court, the pool is secured by a lightly-scaled wrought iron gate and fence capped with wood. Planting softens the stonework: *Begonia grandis* (hardy begonia) edges the bluestone walk while *Perovskia atriplicifolia* cascades over the wall at the top of the steps. Photographs by Michael McKinley.

Overleaf: The iced driveway looks like a frozen stream flowing through a balance of deciduous and evergreen plants. Across the drive, *Panicum virgatum* 'Haense Herms' is weighted down by the snow, which caps the adjacent deadheads of *Sedum* x *telephium* 'Autumn Joy'. Several *Ilex* x *attenuata* 'Fosteri' provide an evergreen transition to the scale of deciduous woodland. *Liriope muscari* 'Big Blue' is a foil to the triumphant forms of *Yucca filamentosa,* which set off the golden *Miscanthus sinensis gracillimus*. Photograph by Caroline Segui-Kosar.

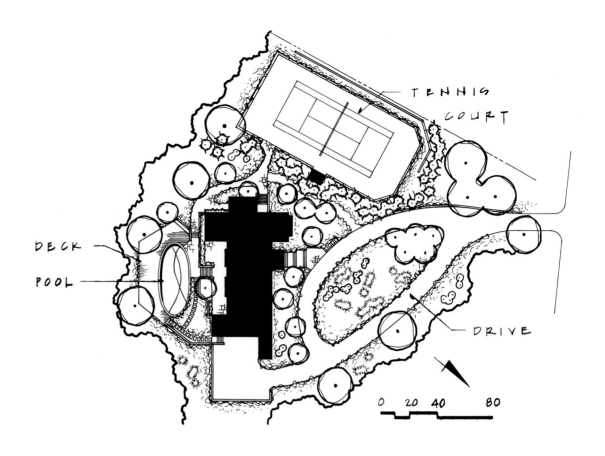

TENNIS COURT

DECK

POOL

DRIVE

0 20 40   80

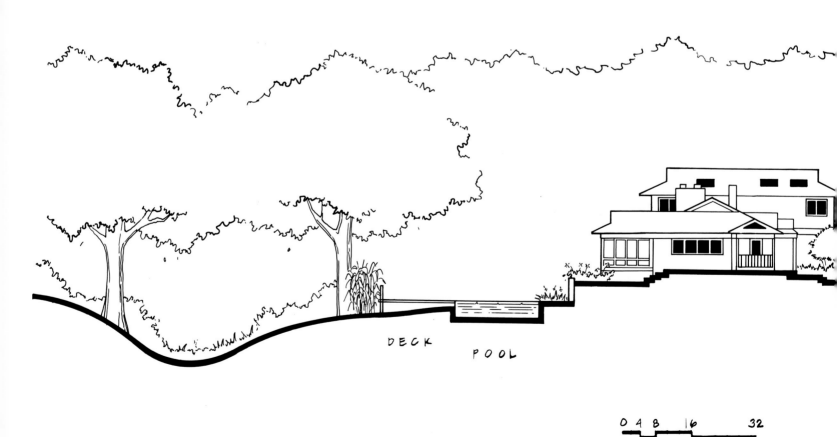

DECK   POOL

0 4 8 16   32

The tennis court is obscured from the house by *Ilex* x *attenuata* 'Fosteri' and deciduous azaleas, underplanted with *Sedum* x 'Ruby Glow'. The architect designed a shed for tennis equipment to match the house. Photograph by Michael McKinley.

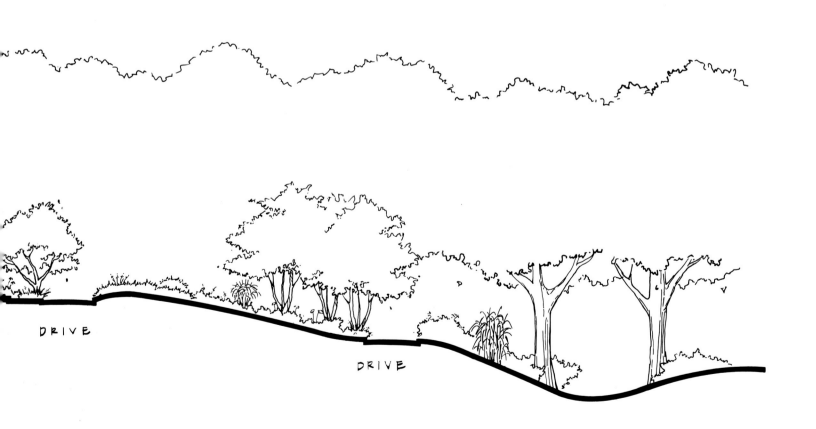

DRIVE

DRIVE

The International Center on a 28-acre site in northwest Washington, D.C. has been developed by the United States Department of State for 22 foreign chancelleries. Eight acres are devoted to public gardens of which we designed three distinct areas in consecutive stages with perhaps 750,000 plants in all. The Southwest Quadrant (see page 262) is a buffer zone between a public street and the south side of the International Center. The two-acre Central Park (opposite) presented an existing monumental stone staircase and retaining walls to which we responded with more than 19,000 plants. The neighboring INTELSAT headquarters dominates the background. Photograph by John Neubauer.

The 1½-acre Northwest Quadrant creates a holding pond as required by city law to hold three feet of water for 45 minutes in the event of a rainfall which may occur once every ten years. We turned what could have been an unsightly drainage pit into a sunken garden which is enjoyed by neighborhood residents and embassy employees alike. A foreground planting of *Hosta* x 'Honeybells' is silhouetted against a floor of lawn and grove of *Taxodium distichum* (bald cypress) which are enjoying the moist conditions so much that they are developing "knees"— very unusual in a garden situation. The brilliant *Lythrum salicaria* 'Morden's Pink' cascades down the slope, with the creamy plumes of *Cortaderia selloana pumila* standing out along the top. Photograph by Michael McKinley.

DESIGNS FOR NEIGHBORS

The Draper and Smith Gardens

Opposite: The Smith (left) and Draper
residences exemplify the Federal period of early 19th
century Georgetown. A historic iron fence frames
the streetside entrance to the Smith Garden.
The Drapers' parking bay is visible just beyond the
Smiths' front steps. *Above:* Through the Drapers'
gate, the "traditional" Georgetown garden
is very tidy, with a teak bench and potted
annuals. The doorsill was made from a granite carriage
stone found in the old garden.
Photographs by Michael McKinley.

An opportunity to design gardens for adjacent Federal-period townhouses led to a unified public face and very different private domains behind brick walls. Georgetown is an enclave of the Capitol City, its trove of historic architecture closely guarded by the National Commission of Fine Arts. The Commission must approve any changes within view of the street, including facades, entrances, fences, walls, gates, and parking, for compatibility with the Georgetown idiom.

The Draper garden set the precedents for the streetside treatment. Phyllis Draper chose the black-green paint for woodwork which is traditional to the Georgetown Federal house. We extended an existing brick wall to carve a parking bay out of the original driveway entrance, while giving over the rest of the driveway to garden space.

The Smiths agreed to unify the two facades with fences, gates, tongue-and-groove woodwork, and paint color. Although the Drapers' imposing, handsome front door opens onto high steps, the Smiths' entrance was minimal and hard—just two granite steps and a bare sidewalk. Planters now flank the door and soften the steps. We had to remove part of an old iron fence along the sidewalk to give access to the Smith's new parking bay. Once restored, the typical Georgetown "speared" fence was reconnected as a "return" along the drive toward the wooden fence.

Right: To soften the austere stoop of the Smith residence, we flanked it with two custom-made planters which cascade with *Lamiastrum galeobdolon* (yellow archangel) and *Pieris japonica* (lily-of-the-valley bush). *Lamiastrum*'s silvered edge and the colorful *Impatiens* cultivar added by Niente Smith brighten the deeply shaded entrance. Photograph by James van Sweden.

Opposite above: The upper level of the
Draper Garden is designed as a receiving room for
parties given on the much larger lower
terrace. A *Styrax japonicus* (Japanese snowbell) shelters
the bench and defines the edge of the upper space.
Planting beds are edged in brick; the herringbone-
patterned paving visually expands the space.
Above: On axis with a venerable *Salix babylonica*
(weeping willow), the dark blue swimming
pool is like a mirror. The intersection of various
levels is articulated by small trees. An *Acer
palmatum* (Japanese maple) stands to the right of the
broad steps to the upper terrace; opposite, a
Magnolia virginiana flanks wooden steps leading up to
the living room and provides a canopy for the
lower level entrance to the dining room. Along the
pool, the flower color of *Lythrum salicaria* 'Morden's
Pink' is echoed by *Lagerstroemia indica* (crape
myrtle). Photographs by Michael McKinley.

Seen from the living room porch, the
terrace was designed to accommodate up to 150
guests for cocktails or seat 40 at dinner.
Its main feature is an S-curve, incorporating a semi-
circular bench. To the right of the steps ascending from
the dining room below is a *Magnolia* x *soulangiana*
(saucer magnolia), underplanted with *Brunnera
macrophylla* and *Galium odoratum* (sweet woodruff).
A *Cornus kousa* in the middle of the terrace
is surrounded with *Liriope muscari* 'Big Blue'. Brick
walls are softened by *Cotoneaster salicifolius
repens* on the bottom left, and an
old-fashioned white climbing *Rosa* on the right.
Photograph by Michael McKinley.

In spring, the Draper Garden is ringed
with the clear bright hues of *Tulipa* 'Emperor' cultivars.
Around the rear perimeter, privacy plantings of
Ilex opaca (American holly) and *Tsuga canadensis*
(Canada hemlock) work with the neighbor's
handsome stand of *Phyllostachys* (bamboo).
Photograph by Valerie Brown.

0 8 10 20 40

POOL

POOL

LAWN

TERRACE

VERANDA

PARKING

STREET

Guests enjoy a view across the pool to the
old-fashioned border. *Coreopsis verticillata* 'Moonbeam'
lights up the area in front of the bench; the intense
hue of *Liatris spicata* is extended by *Lythrum
salicaria* 'Morden's Pink' which gives height at the
corner of the pool. Note the patina
on the brick terrace which was laid in sand.
Photograph by Michael McKinley.

Preceding page: Fringed with *Wisteria sinensis* (Chinese wisteria), a covered porch feels like country in the city. Beyond, from left to right, are the small formal lawn with perennial borders, swimming pool and carriage house for guests. Photograph by Volkmar Wentzel.

"The garden means beauty and peace in the midst of the city. Favorite plants are the flowering perennials that reintroduce themselves and surprise me season by season."
—Phyllis C. Draper

"We really have three gardens in one, which is quite remarkable for such a small space. In addition to the perennial borders and pool, there is a casual play area with a sandbox and trees for climbing. It's very important to have a garden that my son can use and yet which is very much for us, too."
—Niente I. Smith

Opposite above: Looking at the view through a rather traditional planting toward the guest house, you might not even know the swimming pool is there. The planting design complements an existing old-fashioned single rose with *Liatris spicata* and *Phlox* cultivar, under the branch of a *Malus* cultivar (crab apple). *Opposite below:* A traditional latticework screens the parking court from the garden proper. This segment of the perennial border combines *Rudbeckia fulgida* 'Goldsturm' with *Hosta* x 'Honeybells'. Climbing *Parthenocissus tricuspidata* (Boston ivy) cloaks the house next door and blurs the border between. *Above:* An automated double gate opens to the Smiths' two parking spaces, screened from the street by a six-foot fence. Photographs by Michael McKinley.

Beyond the unified public view, through the garden gates, exist two different, private worlds. Each is attuned to the English-spirited Federal architecture in a formal way, since neither the Drapers nor the Smiths perceived the city garden as a meadow of ornamental grasses.

The Draper garden design dramatizes the act of arrival and entry for their guests. For parties, the parking bay doubles as an antechamber, from which you pass through a gate into the upper level or foyer, conceived as a traditional Georgetown garden. The pool, which already existed, is an axial centerpiece that captures daylight within the enclosure. Down broad steps, a large terrace accommodates three or four tables, each seating ten for dinner. Big pillows add comfort to the sinuous bench which frames the terrace. Bold pots filled with annuals satisfy the Drapers' Californian love of bold color which is otherwise hard to achieve in Washington, D.C.

The Smiths' tastes were more restrained, tending toward an "English" border, highly styled. This is a garden for children and family, so the border surrounds a little lawn for throwing a ball or a frisbee. In contrast to the axial Draper garden, we screened this swimming pool from the entry by a high-backed bench tucked into the flowers at the lawn's edge. A charming veranda, lined with window-boxes of *Pelargonium* species (red geraniums) and *Senecio cineraria* (dusty-miller), surveys the entire garden, from "English" bordered lawn to pool, swing and sandbox.

AN APARTMENT TERRACE

This terrace garden extends the livable space of a two-story condominium in a large apartment complex in Washington, D.C. It happens to be a roof garden over the parking garage, so all plants had to be chosen for shallow root systems and suitability for container planting. A gas grill is set into a granite counter, with a nearby pot of herbs for cooking and scenting the terrace: *Thymus* x *citriodorus* (lemon-scented thyme), *Petroselinum crispum* (parsley) and *Anethum graveolens* (dill) accented by the red flowers of miniature tropical *Hibiscus.* Behind the herbs, *Coreopsis verticillata* 'Moonbeam' and *Pennisetum alopecuroides* are growing in a raised bed. At the corner near the hammock, a circular redwood container holds a *Maackia amurensis* underplanted with *Gerbera jamesonii* (gerbera daisy) and *Hedera* cultivar (variegated ivy). *Panicum virgatum* 'Haense Herms' is massed in a raised planter over cabinets at the terrace's far end. Photograph by Michael McKinley.

A Henry Moore bronze, "Torso," (1964)
and opposing *Pinus thunbergiana* subdivide the
linear space of this city terrace. Soon to be covered with
Wisteria floribunda (Japanese wisteria) and
Clematis cultivars, the trellis casts shadows on the
existing quarry tile floor—a layer of visual
interest that is continually shifting, disappearing and
reappearing. Turn-of-the-century French armchairs of
wood and iron are from the Vichy casino.
Photograph by Peter Jones.

A MANHATTAN TERRACE

The Rosenberg Terrace

This is a place of controlled views, at once screened for privacy and focused on the Manhattan "cityscape." The design was also governed by the many laws regarding what a designer can do on a 12th-floor roof: containers must be nine inches from the parapet, several inches off the floor and movable. Weight and size are also restricted.

A lightly scaled arbor with lattice side-screens gives privacy from nearby buildings with overhead views. Within, the arbor subdivides the extremely long and narrow terrace, converting it from corridor into a series of "rooms" at human-scale. Low voltage lighting, concealed in the arbor beams overhead, downlights the red quarry tile floor. Eventually, as the arbor drips with green vines, it will become a strong extension of the greenhouse to which it is attached.

With such a long garden, designed to be seen from one end, layers create depth and enticement. Here the layering of plants begins in the greenhouse with a very interesting French plant stand, chosen by interior designer Andrée Putman. In the middle distance, a bronze torso by Henry Moore is a major focal point, while trees in containers step back toward the end of the terrace, where diners enjoy views of midtown Manhattan and Central Park.

Lattice is used to screen the terrace from buildings across the alley; here it is repeated against the opposite brick wall to relieve its enormous and monotonous scale. Shadowplay on the wall, a few inches behind, gives added dimension. Photograph by Peter Jones.

A welded aluminum wall sculpture,
"Ashasuerus' Decree" by David Jacobs (1988),
gives life and sparkle to the brick wall and visually
connects with the skyline and tempo of midtown
Manhattan. Restored vintage French parc
chairs surround the dining table, set against a parapet
planting of *Pennisetum viridescens* (purple
fountain grass) underlining the vista.
Photograph by Peter Jones.

Above: The Rosenbergs' dining room window is an object lesson in transforming the most limited view into an evocative scene. Within the high-gloss frame, layering begins with an art deco silverplate tea set with ebony handles (Christofle, Paris) and George Segal's "Girl Meditating," (cast resin, 1975). Just beyond the transparent screen, the parapet is planted like a dish garden, with *Pinus thunbergiana* (Japanese black pine), *Lamiastrum galeobdolon* (yellow archangel), and *Panicum virgatum* 'Haense Herms'. Interior designed by Andrée Putman. *Below:* From the garden room, the main terrace seems to be in another world. The arbor's slant minimizes what could be a "railroad car" quality; and the arrangement of potted plants in layers, beginning inside with a Parisian plant stand (ca. 1880), encourages the eye to move in a diagonal line across the space. Photographs by Peter Jones

"The terrace combines a country feeling with a city view to create a dimension that I have never before experienced. Likewise, sitting in the solarium's summer atmosphere, I don't forget that it's winter. Rather, it creates *another* season for me. Those dimensions are what the garden is all about."
—Alex Rosenberg

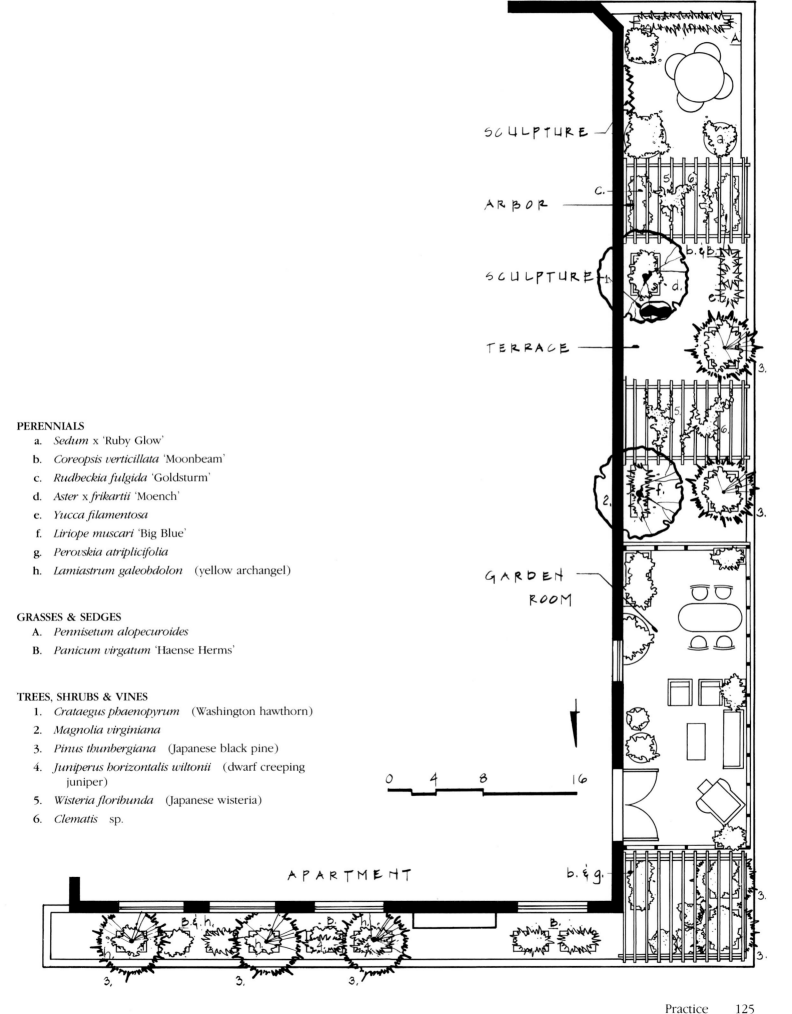

PERENNIALS

    a. *Sedum* x 'Ruby Glow'

    b. *Coreopsis verticillata* 'Moonbeam'

    c. *Rudbeckia fulgida* 'Goldsturm'

    d. *Aster* x *frikartii* 'Moench'

    e. *Yucca filamentosa*

    f. *Liriope muscari* 'Big Blue'

    g. *Perovskia atriplicifolia*

    h. *Lamiastrum galeobdolon*   (yellow archangel)

GRASSES & SEDGES

    A. *Pennisetum alopecuroides*

    B. *Panicum virgatum* 'Haense Herms'

TREES, SHRUBS & VINES

    1. *Crataegus phaenopyrum* (Washington hawthorn)

    2. *Magnolia virginiana*

    3. *Pinus thunbergiana* (Japanese black pine)

    4. *Juniperus horizontalis wiltonii* (dwarf creeping juniper)

    5. *Wisteria floribunda* (Japanese wisteria)

    6. *Clematis* sp.

SCULPTURE

ARBOR

SCULPTURE

TERRACE

GARDEN ROOM

APARTMENT

0   4   8   16

Practice   125

THE GARDEN AS FRAME

The walled garden of Mrs. John Nef is the frame for a 1971 work by Marc Chagall. Made of natural stone from Italy's Cararra region and glass from Murano, the mosaic is an allegory celebrating the pilgrims' journey to America; it includes Pegasus and the Three Graces soaring overhead, as well as Mr. and Mrs. Nef themselves. From the loggia, the view is framed by *Wisteria* and an old-fashioned soft pink climbing cabbage *Rosa.* This Washington, D.C., shade garden is understated in color and design; the pea gravel terrace, bordered with red brick, does not compete with the mosaic. Photograph by Michael McKinley.

PUBLIC GARDEN IN THE CAPITAL CITY

The Federal Reserve Garden

Opposite: Yucca filamentosa's bold lines offer a stiff contrast to the feathery quality of *Calamagrostis acutiflora stricta,* achieving balance between evergreen structure and dried winter perennials. (Photograph by Volkmar Wentzel.)
Above: The Martin Building's east facade, as an automobile passenger would see it when approaching from the Washington Monument. *Miscanthus sinensis gracillimus,* in a sea of *Rudbeckia fulgida* 'Goldsturm', frames the fountain. Photograph by Michael McKinley.

A dramatic view of the Washington Monument says it all about this public garden within five blocks of the White House. The Federal Reserve Garden injects human comfort and informal drama into the most formal urban landscape in America. Built on the roof of an underground parking garage, the garden surrounds the 'Seventies-era Martin Building, an annex of the Federal Reserve.

When a severe winter killed some ninety percent of the site's original regimental evergreens, David Lilly of the Federal Reserve Board of Governors took responsibility for improving the landscape. He asked for sitting areas of human scale so people could escape from the overpowering, monumental city, especially important in the summer. At the Federal Reserve Garden, you can be sheltered by plants, have a sense of privacy and contact with nature.

The underground garage structure allowed 18 inches of soil for planting perennials and lawn, and four-foot mounds for trees. We used the mounds and existing planters to sculpt the ground plane, channeling the view across the central lawn toward the Martin Building. Sitting areas on either side are screened for privacy and protection by profuse plantings and earth berms. Shade trees cool these alcoves, which sometimes act as galleries for small sculptures. Toward the side street, tennis courts are screened by planted berms.

Late autumn. Photograph by Michael McKinley.

PERENNIALS
- **a.** *Bergenia cordifolia*
- **b.** *Liriope muscari* 'Big Blue'
- **c.** *Epimedium* x *versicolor* (long-spur epimedium)

GRASSES & SEDGES
- **A.** *Miscanthus sinensis gracillimus*
- **B.** *Calamagrostis acutiflora stricta*
- **C.** *Pennisetum alopecuroides*

TREES & SHRUBS
1. *Zelkova serrata*
2. *Sophora japonica*
3. *Quercus rubra*
4. *Quercus phellos*

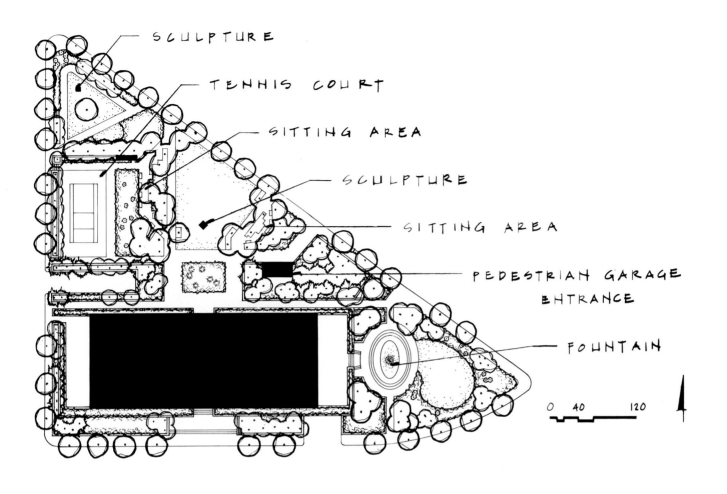

SCULPTURE

TENNIS COURT

SITTING AREA

SCULPTURE

SITTING AREA

PEDESTRIAN GARAGE ENTRANCE

FOUNTAIN

0   40   120

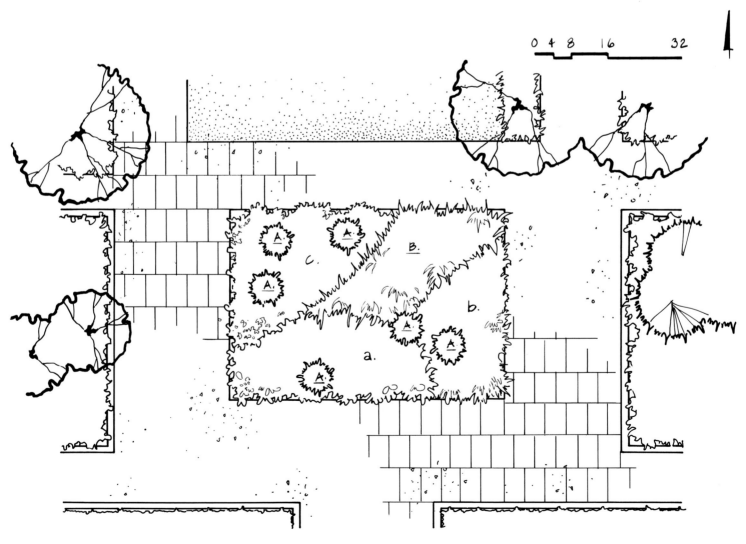

0 4 8 16   32

A
A
C
B
A
b
A
a
A

"The symbolism and imagery of the Federal
Reserve Landscape have had a tremendous
impact on the environment of Washington, D.C.
Hopefully, it seems to be moving away from
the aristocratic European model toward a
reflection of the egalitarian United States and
its Great Plains heritage."
—David M. Lilly

While the landscape design locates the individual within the experience of a garden, it also situates the building within the L'Enfant plan of the capital city. The main vista was shaped by Washington's unusual urban framework of diagonal and right-angled streets. Though the Martin Building fronts on the diagonal Virginia Avenue, it lines up with the square grid of Constitution Avenue and C Street behind it. Thus do the two sidewalks flanking the central lawn angle toward the entry from Virginia Avenue, asymmetrically forcing the perspective and reconciling the diagonal to the square.

Both the central and the side lawns were scaled to set off the building and display large sculptures. Thousands of perennials, including *Rudbeckia fulgida* 'Goldsturm', frame the side lawn and give privacy from the public sidewalk. The front lawn, on the other hand, acts as a foil to a massive square planting bed directly in front of the main entry. This is quite similar in concept, if not in scale, to the way we handle residential front yards, creating a screening layer between the street and the front door. At the Federal Reserve, this scales down the building and deflects pedestrians to the right or the left walkway. Uncharacteristically, we retained existing planters of pruned *Ilex crenata* (Japanese holly) to ease the transition from architecture to garden. Like green marble, the hedge helps this building meet its new landscape more effectively.

A first for the capital landscape, this garden found its perfect champion in David Lilly. Its critics claimed that the proposed design was too natural and too residential, with too many different plants and spaces. The prevailing attitude of the time was to keep Washington, D.C., very prim, pressed and starched. Indeed, the traditional capitol landscape is impressive and imposing. But the pertinent question is whether to reinforce or counteract that. As a great gardener himself, David Lilly was able to persuade both the Board of Governors and the National Commission of Fine Arts that a garden design which was atypical of the public landscape was exactly what was needed.

At first, the people who worked in the Martin Building thought the newly installed garden plants looked like weeds. Extraordinary applications of fish emulsion helped it to grow rapidly and luxuriantly. Only 40 people were expected when we gave a lunchtime lecture-tour to explain the garden, but 400 came. Now they say that they can not imagine life without the garden.

Above: The Board of Governors of the Federal Reserve System wanted a garden that would be welcoming in the monumental scale of Washington, D.C.—a place where people could relax, enjoy and discover plants. *Rudbeckia fulgida* 'Goldsturm' in the foreground is overhung with the foliage of *Zelkova serrata; Sophora japonica* (Japanese pagoda tree) across the lawn are in full flower. As a sculpture by Sol Lewitt demonstrates, the main lawn is designed for changing exhibits of large sculpture; walkways frame the lawn on all sides. Photograph by Michael McKinley.

Below: Looking from Virginia Avenue toward the north front of the Martin Building, it is hard to imagine that the garden is atop a parking garage because the ground plane is at the same level as the public sidewalk. An existing hedge of *Ilex crenata* (Japanese holly) is a tailored foil to the loose textures of the rectangular planting bed, featuring *Calamagrostis acutiflora stricta, Epimedium* x *versicolor* and *Miscanthus sinsensis gracillimus* in late summer. Photograph by James van Sweden.

Since 1981, we have been working with the Pennsylvania Avenue Development Corporation, Washington, D.C. It was President John F. Kennedy who instigated the project, which includes plazas by Carol Johnson, M. Paul Friedberg and Robert Venturi. Our assignment has been planting design from the National Treasury to the National Gallery. We have given these 12 blocks a unified image, introducing the character of one kind of garden throughout. Left: This view from Freedom Plaza looks toward the U.S. Capitol dome. Alcoves surround the entire Plaza like show windows that can be read from an automobile. We have arranged each "window" with collections of plants in various and interesting combinations. This particular alcove contains *Calamagrostis acutiflora stricta, Caryopteris* x *clandonensis* and *Coreopsis verticillata* 'Moonbeam'. Photograph by Michael McKinley.

Opposite: Detail of an alcove and one of the succession of pedestals supporting the great aluminum urns designed by Robert Venturi. In early autumn, this urn is topped off with *Yucca pendula* in the center drum, circled with orange *Lantana camara* (yellow sage) which is interspersed with yellow *Tagetes* hybrid (marigolds). Silhouetted against the pink marble walls of the alcove is the fiery fall color of *Miscanthus sinensis purpurascens,* with *Sedum* x *telephium* 'Autumn Joy' and *Ceratostigma plumbaginoides* in the foreground. On the left is the red-tipped foliage of *Nandina domestica.* Photograph by Volkmar Wentzel.

At the project's eastern end, new plantings enliven a traffic island centering on Major General George Gordon Meade, a Civil War hero of Gettysburg, by Charles A. Grafly. A regiment of *Tulipa* hybrids occupies the space in spring, with the lily-flowering 'Marietta' in the foreground. Photograph by Carol M. Highsmith.

The same view in mid-summer shows how dramatic seasonal changes come to Pennsylvania Avenue, with *Coreopsis verticillata* 'Moonbeam', *Yucca filamentosa* and *Eupatorium purpureum* 'Gateway'. Photograph by Michael McKinley.

WOODLAND CLEARING

The Shockey Garden

*I*n Virginia's wooded countryside, a striking new home had been abruptly cut into a hill. It faced due south for passive heat gain, but otherwise neglected the setting. It was all the more disturbing to come upon this gleaming, modern concrete house after the rustic experience of the gravel drive, threading between woods and apple orchards.

Mr. Shockey, a leading concrete supplier, wished to develop the property to showcase his company's product. The Shockeys were not avid gardeners and did not have a specific idea of what they wanted to do with the landscape, but they knew they had a problem. Giving the house a setting was the clear goal. It required extensive regrading to overcome the void between the house, which jutted out of a filled earth bank, and the natural contour.

We overcame a 21-foot drop between the entry court and entertainment terrace with a dramatic waterfall and winding stair. At the top, near the front door, a quiet lily pool drops six feet into a "cauldron" so deep that the echoing waters can only be heard, not seen. It signals entry into the more private world of the garden proper. At a resting point halfway down the stairs, a wide landing adjoins a still pool before it hastens on in a cascade toward the large pool at the bottom, on the entertainment terrace. We placed a few boulders along the hillside between the woodland edge and the staircase to better knit the waterfall into the landscape.

Opposite: Light filters down onto the Shockeys' lily pool, edged with the dish-like leaves of *Nelumbo nucifera* (sacred lotus) and the spidery mid-summer flowers of *Thalia dealbata* (water canna). Overhanging the water on the left, behind *Sagittaria latifolia* (common arrowhead), is *Eupatorium purpureum* 'Gateway'. *Above:* Arrival at the Shockeys' private cul-de-sac is like coming upon a clearing in the woods. Autumn's burnished colors are set off by the pristinely stuccoed house.
Photographs by Michael McKinley.

Winter opens the garden to the pasture
beyond the woods and the distant horizon—the
limits of the view. The drive enters this scene like a
country road, marked on the right by a spot
of green *Fargesia nitida* and, on the left, a stand of
Miscanthus sinensis purpurascens amidst
Sedum x *telephium* 'Autumn Joy'. Leaves of *Thalia
dealbata* hover like sheets of tarnished
silver above the frozen water. Photograph by
Caroline Segui-Kosar.

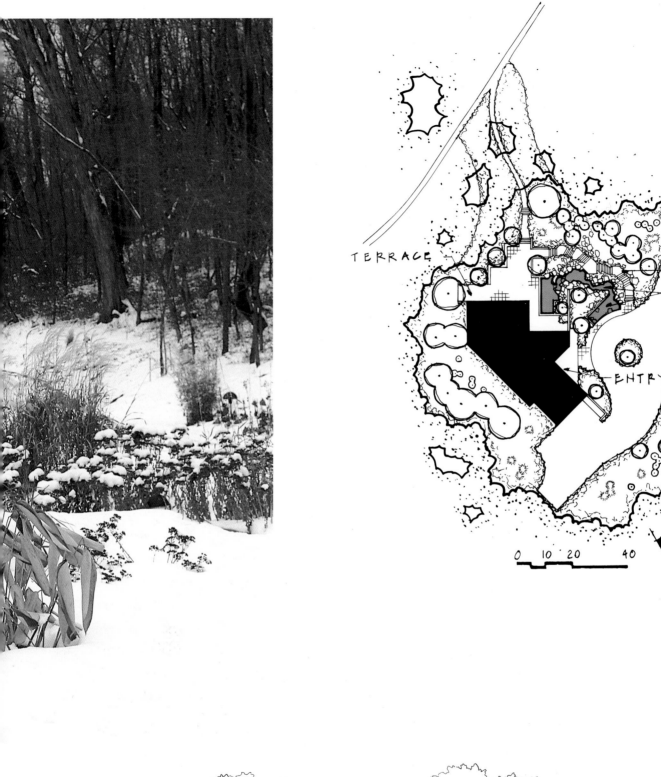

TERRACE

STEPS
LILY
POOLS

ENTRY

0 10 20   40

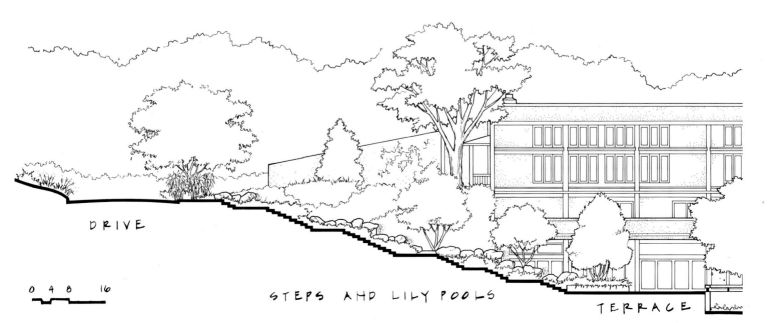

DRIVE

0 4 8   16

STEPS AND LILY POOLS

TERRACE

View from the top of the slope shows the
checkerboard-patterned terrace 22 feet below, surfaced
with beige-tinted precast pavers and visually
defined by a built-in bench. Mid-summer blooms
include the bright pink of *Aster* x *frikartii*
'Moench', against the darker rose of
Eupatorium purpureum 'Gateway' across the waterfall.
Sedum x *telephium* 'Autumn Joy' is forming its
broccoli heads. *Betula nigra* (river birch) relates to the
water while partially screening the lower terrace.
Photograph by Michael McKinley.

In absolute contrast to the clean white
concrete walls, the waterfall climaxes as it sheets
off a rock ledge into the lowest pool at bench height.
Photograph by Michael McKinley.

Mid-summer. Photograph by Michael McKinley.

PERENNIALS

a. *Sedum* x *telephium* 'Autumn Joy'

b. *Coreopsis verticillata* 'Moonbeam'

c. *Liatris spicata*

d. *Astilbe* sp. (false spirea)

e. *Lamiastrum galeobdolon* (yellow archangel)

f. *Hemerocallis* sp. (daylily)

g. *Dryopteris* sp. (wood fern)

h. *Ligularia dentata* 'Desdemona'

i. *Geranium endressii* 'Wargrave Pink' (cranesbill)

j. *Iris sibirica* (Siberian iris)

k. *Aster* x *frikartii* 'Moench'

l. *Artemisia ludoviciana* 'Silver-King'

m. *Perovskia atriplicifolia*

n. *Acanthus hungaricus*

o. *Hosta* x 'Honeybells' (plantain lily)

p. *Liriope muscari* 'Big Blue'

q. *Eupatorium purpureum* 'Gateway'

r. *Rudbeckia fulgida* 'Goldsturm'

s. *Lythrum salicaria* 'Morden's Pink'

t. *Bergenia cordifolia*

u. *Sagittaria latifolia* (common arrowhead)

v. *Pontederia cordata* (pickerelweed)

w. *Iris sibirica* 'Caesar's Brother' (Siberian iris)

x. *Lobelia cardinalis* (cardinal flower)

y. *Nelumbo nucifera* (sacred lotus)

GRASSES & SEDGES

A. *Deschampsia caespitosa*

B. *Pennisetum alopecuroides viridescens* (dark blooming fountain grass)

C. *P. orientale* (orient fountain grass)

D. *Panicum virgatum* 'Haense Herms'

E. *Miscanthus sinensis gracillimus*

F. *Phyllostachys aureosulcata* (yellow-groove bamboo)

G. *Spodiopogon sibiricus*

TREES & SHRUBS

1. *Ilex opaca* (American holly)

2. *Betula nigra* (river birch)

3. *Fargesia nitida*

4. *Zelkova serrata* 'Greenvase'

5. *Magnolia virginiana*

6. *Pinus bungeana* (lace-bark pine)

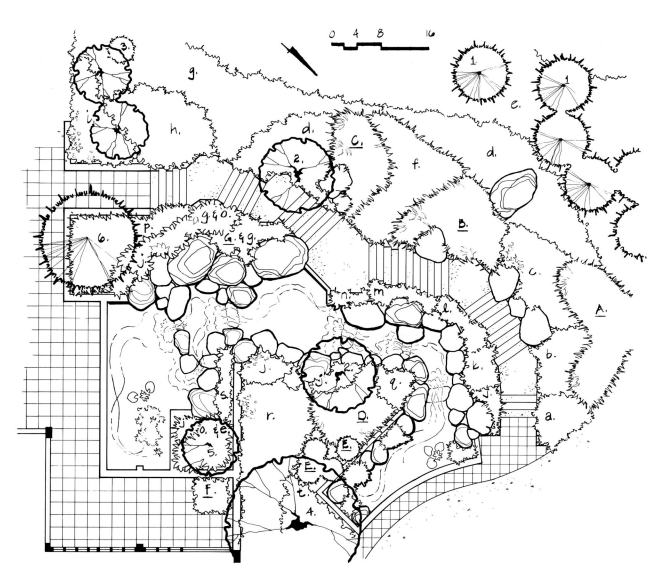

Echoing the water cascade, 42 staggered
steps let plants such as *Hosta* x 'Honeybells' and the
silvery *Artemisia ludoviciana* 'Silver-King' (white sage)
splash over the edges to soften the architecture.
To create a rough-hewn riser, a mold was
taken from a carved limestone step, then the steps were
cast in concrete and tinted beige to match the
lighter pavers of the terrace. On the far
right, a *Pinus bungeana* (lace-bark
pine) is underplanted with *Liriope muscari* 'Big
Blue'. Photograph by Michael McKinley.

"The garden brings warmth to the house and makes it belong to the woods and surrounding landscape. The constant change throughout the seasons is like a kaleidoscope. Each morning we get up and look out the window and see something we haven't seen before."
—Shirley and Donald Shockey

Attention to details of fit included tapering the garage wall to follow the roof line down to the ground as a screen for the service court. To make the 21-foot slope seem less formidable, the steps are generously sized at six feet wide. A built-in bench zig-zags along the outer edge of the lower terrace, reiterating the modernist lines of the house while protecting people from the steep slope below.

Another flight of wide steps leads from the lower terrace toward the woods. What had been a service road for construction was adjusted to lead the eye along a woodland path. It is planted to evoke Thomas Jefferson's gardens at Monticello in the spring, with *Cornus kousa, Cercis canadensis* (redbud), *Ilex opaca* (American holly), *Rhododendron* and *Azalea* species blooming at the same time as the groundcover of *Galium odoratum* (sweet woodruff), *Vinca minor* (common periwinkle), *Osmunda cinnamomea* (cinnamon fern) and spring bulbs.

Color also plays a part. The planting design makes a transition from a bright, meadow-like border along the driveway into more detailed, subdued planting along the waterfall. A play of blues between the stairs and the waterfall uses *Artemisia* 'Silver King' and 'Silver Mound', *Aster* x *frikartii* 'Moench', *Acanthus hungaricus* and *Ceratostigma plumbaginoides*. An earthy tint in the checkerboard terrace paving and the sidewalk to the front door helps bring the woodland floor into the garden, allaying the stark white architecture.

Although the site is a woodland clearing, the treeline is actually at a considerable distance from the house. Newly planted flowering trees and shrubs fill the gap, seeming to emerge from existing specimens further back in the woods. This understory helps bring the scale down from 40-foot trees to human size and creates a natural break between the sunny perennials that border the waterfall and the shady garden that filters into this woodland setting.

The Jacobs Garden in Washington, D.C., yields flowers, fruit and foliage for Gail Jacobs' work in floral design. Stone terraces step down a gentle slope from the house toward a swimming pool and pergola, all designed in an earlier phase by Lester Collins. We were brought in to further develop the property, extend the perennial gardens and design the lily pool. Photograph by Michael McKinley.

The bouquet is gathered from the late summer garden. In the center are the red berries of *Aralia racemosa,* set off by a white *Lilium* cultivar. Other blossoms include the light pink of *Anemone hupehensis* (Japanese anemone) with yellow centers; the bright yellow of a double *Coreopsis* cultivar; *Echinacea purpurea* (purple coneflower) is pink with an orange-brown center; and the delicate hanging pink flowers of *Begonia grandis* (hardy begonia). *Typha angustifolia* (narrow-leaf cattail) are taken from the lily pool; from nearby come the large leaves of *Ligularia dentata* 'Desdemona'. The golden inflorescence of *Pennisetum alopecuroides* shimmers in the backlight. Arrangement by Gail L. Jacobs Flower Craft. Photograph by Rhoda Baer.

AN OCEAN RETREAT

The Slifka Garden

The secluded Slifka garden is protected
from the Atlantic Ocean winds and salt spray
by a traditional shingled cottage. *Opposite:* In the
foreground is a good seaside plant,
Salvia x *superba* 'Mainacht'. In the distance,
stairs lead to the second-level front door portico.
Above: The view from the veranda shows
that the landside dune was largely left alone.
Both the walkway and the ocean viewing platform
were designed in collaboration with the architect.
Photographs by Michael McKinley.

etween the Atlantic Ocean dunes and potato fields lies a garden which suits both. And like Barbara Slifka's "hurricane room" on the leeward side of the house, this garden protects her from the wind and surrounds her with lush colors and textures.

Our first concern was to improve the relationship between the ground plane and the fanciful house, towering three stories above the narrow lot. The ground floor walls are actually open lattice which sheathes the pilings and changing rooms; shingles clad the upper two stories. We addressed the house itself with a combination of structural strategies. Perhaps most important, an arbor parallels the second floor level along the garden side of the house. As an "eyelid" of green, it brings the house down to human size. The entry, designed in tandem with the architect, grounds the house with broad steps and tall planters. Two flowering trees at the entrance—*Magnolia virginiana* and *Amelanchier canadensis*—also ease the transition from house to human scale.

Native plants, lighting and sightlines fit the garden within the larger landscape. Overall, we took a loose, unfussy approach, relying heavily on grasses and foliage plants. Along the driveway, broad-brush plantings are extremely casual and reminiscent of wildflowers and grasses in roadside verges.

The sun-bleached palette of the seaside is well suited with *Stachys byzantina* (lamb's-ears) in early summer bloom and *Helictotrichon sempervirens'* wands of beige. Built elements, such as the zigzag bench at the end of the pool, are used to tie the house and garden together. Panels of lattice and an "eyelid" of arbor (eventually to cascade with *Polygonum aubertii*) bring the garden up the wall of the house to the first floor. Photograph by Michael McKinley.

A gate leads to the garden proper, which is a compact composition of distinct places and connections. Framed by trees, a "foyer" opens to a corridor leading to the terrace at poolside. The lap pool, 45 feet long, is proportioned and placed to reflect the gable of the house. Distant agricultural rows are recalled by the linearity of fence, pool and paving. At the far end of the pool is a sitting niche designed as a visual destination from the house into the garden. Originally, Barbara Slifka expected to sit mostly on the oceanside deck, which proved to be prohibitively windy at times. Now the niche at poolside is valued as a quiet little garden, where she sits quite often.

Plantings around the pool are more studied than in the entry sequence. *Coreopsis verticillata* 'Moonbeam' and *Salvia* x *superba* 'Mainacht' complement the stained grey fence with strong colors and textures, while cool blue and gray plants seem to extend the space at the far end of the pool. *Perovskia atriplicifolia,* which grows happily in these conditions and accents all the other plants so well, is used throughout to unify the small garden. *Pennisetum alopecuroides* and *Miscanthus sinensis gracillimus* overhang the pool, erasing its hard edge.

We slightly mounded the rear of the garden, tilting the ground plane down toward the pool, to gain privacy. The elevated plantings are revealed as a triangle of *Pinus thunbergiana* (Japanese black pine), *Myrica pensylvanica* (bayberry) and ornamental grasses that seem to swoop down to the house from the surrounding landscape. Mounding relieves the flat natural landform with a visual line that steps up to the sky, accented by vertical plantings that help draw the view.

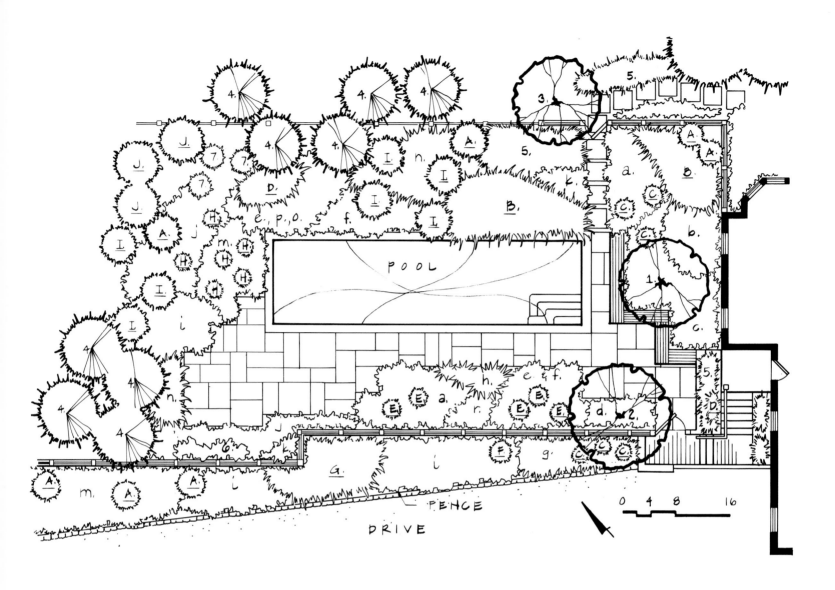

PERENNIALS

a. *Sedum* x *telephium* 'Autumn Joy'

b. *Brunnera macrophylla*

c. *Bergenia cordifolia*

d. *Geranium endressii* 'Wargrave Pink' (cranesbill)

e. *Coreopsis verticillata* 'Moonbeam'

f. *Salvia* x *superba* 'Mainacht'

g. *Liriope muscari* 'Big Blue'

h. *Yucca filamentosa*

i. *Nepeta* x *faassenii* (catnip)

j. *Stachys byzantina* (lamb's-ears)

k. *Hibiscus moscheutos* 'Mixed Colors'

l. *Acanthus hungaricus*

m. *Artemisia schmidtiana* 'Silver Mound'

n. *Hemerocallis* sp. (daylily)

o. *Liatris spicata*

p. *Perovskia atriplicifolia*

q. *Allium giganteum* (giant onion)

r. *Astilbe japonica* 'Deutschland' (Japanese false spirea)

s. *Lantana montevidensis* 'Confetti' (trailing lantana)

GRASSES & SEDGES

A. *Miscanthus sinensis condensatus* (purple-blooming Japanese silver grass)

B. *Pennisetum alopecuroides*

C. *Molinia arundinacea* 'Windspiel' (tall purple moor grass)

D. *Panicum virgatum* 'Haense Herms'

E. *Spodiopogon sibiricus*

F. *Miscanthus sinensis strictus* (porcupine grass)

G. *Sesleria autumnalis*

H. *Helictotrichon sempervirens*

I. *Miscanthus sinensis gracillimus*

J. *M. floridulus*

TREES & SHRUBS

1. *Magnolia virginiana*

2. *Amelanchier canadensis*

3. *Elaeagnus angustifolia* (Russian olive)

4. *Pinus thunbergiana* (Japanese black pine)

5. *Juniperus* sp. (juniper)

6. *Buddleia davidii* (summer lilac)

7. *Myrica pensylvanica* (bayberry)

Early summer. Photograph by Michael McKinley.

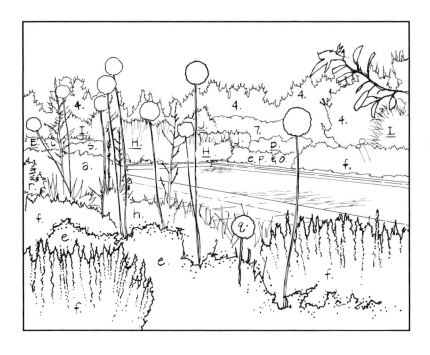

Below right: The view from Barbara Slifka's front door and entrance porch looks north toward the potato fields over the private garden below enclosed by a wall of *Pinus thunbergiana* (black pine). Built on stilts to lift it above the dune, the house also protects the garden from ocean winds. A small sitting alcove, set off from the pool terrace, is a pleasant place for afternoon tea. Photograph by Michael McKinley.

Opposite above: At the shallow end of the swimming pool, steps are treated as a sculptural element. The second step is extended as a bench on which to sit and dangle your legs.
Opposite below: In late summer, the bamboo-like leaves of *Spodiopogon sibiricus* and tendrils of *Clematis paniculata* frame the view over the driveway fence toward the mounded planting area enclosing the pool. To the left of Hilda Steckel's terracotta sculpture, the *Helictotrichon's* blue-gray pin-cushion form is very beachy. A large, light green mound of *Miscanthus sinensis condensatus* rises above the *Stachys byzantina*. Photographs by James van Sweden.

On the dune side, large *P. thunbergiana* grow at the end of the boardwalk as a windbreak, accent and gateway to a little sitting area. We embellished existing dune-side vegetation with *Rosa rugosa* (rugosa rose), *Carex flacca* (sedge), *Panicum virgatum, Gaillardia* x *grandiflora* (blanket flower) and *Prunus maritima* (beach plum).

Without night lighting, anyone would have felt uncomfortably surrounded by a sea of darkness because the house is so high above ground. Instead, looking down upon the garden at night is like viewing an illuminated *bas relief.* Among the dunes, lights beckon to the murmuring surf.

"Every week there are new delights, new surprises and new colors—even the scale as it grows from small bulbs to huge grasses. Each season brings a different visual thrill."
—Barbara Slifka

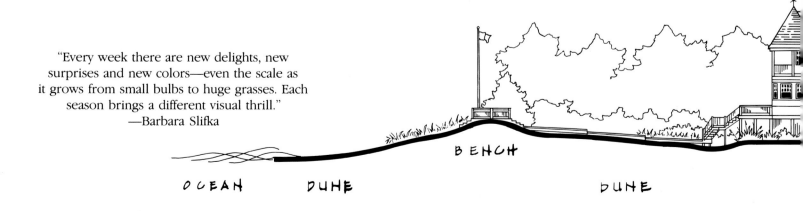

OCEAN   DUNE   BENCH   DUNE

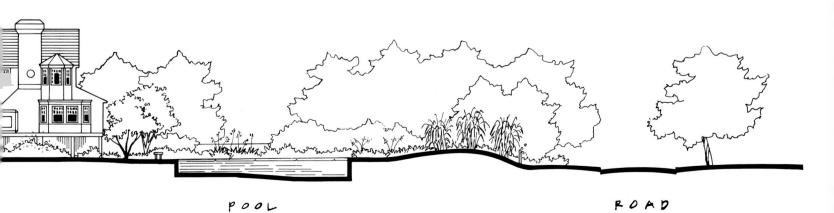

POOL

ROAD

0 4 8   16   32

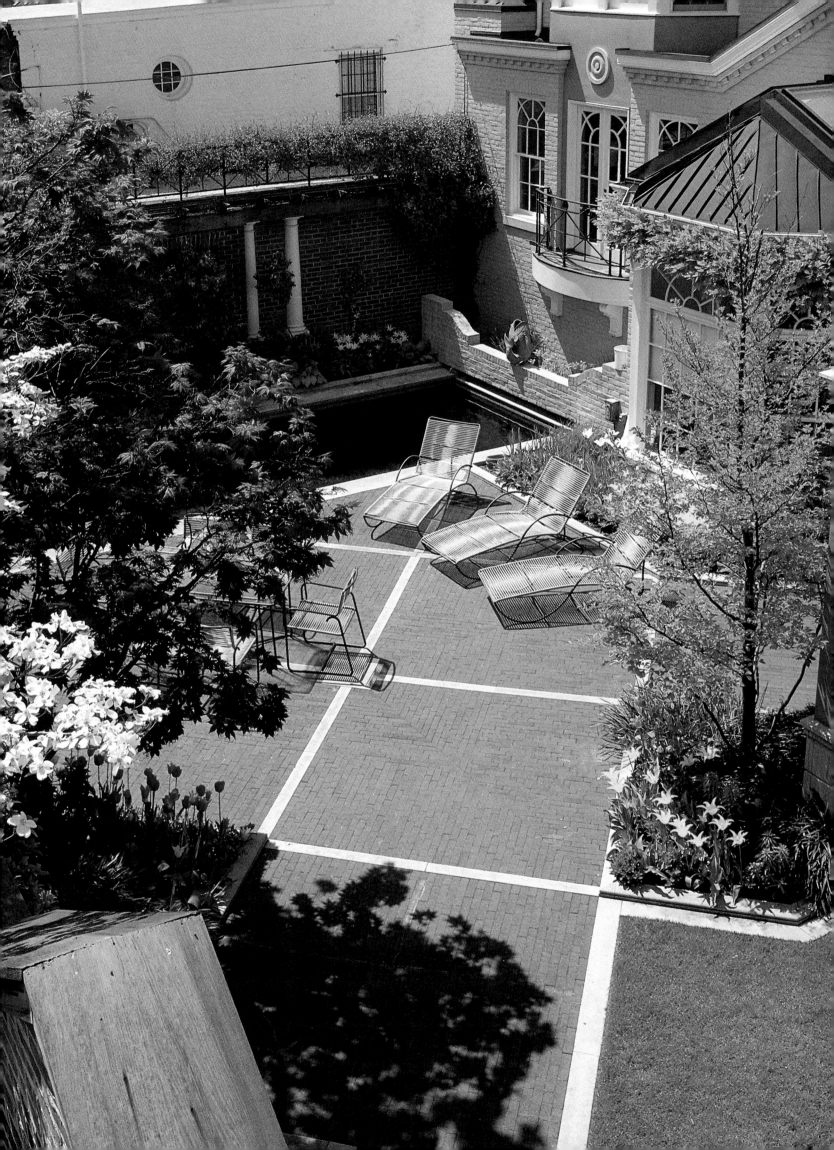

ELEGANCE IN DETAIL

The Schneiderman Garden

Opposite: A spring view from the second floor of the guest house shows many of the refined details that distinguish the Schneiderman Garden. Intricately patterned brick paving is divided on the diagonal by limestone stringers. To the right, is a *Stewartia pseudocamellia* (Japanese stewartia); on the left, are the new red leaves of the *Acer palmatum* (Japanese maple). *Above:* Spring comes to the public sidewalk, edged with limestone and a narrow planting bed that softens the base of the house.
Photographs by Volkmar Wentzel.

The hallmark of this very small garden is richness of material and attention to detail, carried out at the level of workmanship that an elegant residence demands. The townhouse is on a corner lot in Georgetown. In the narrow space between the pool house and the main house was a swimming pool, which guests would nearly fall into when entering through the gate from the public sidewalk.

Finding a place for a new pool across the back of the garden was one of two key decisions. Our second was using a diagonal line to expand the narrow garden, unify the L-shaped space, and simplify the circulation between the living room, kitchen and poolhouse doors. The solution came from picturing the movements of family and guests in various situations.

The overall goal was to marry architecture to garden, without resorting to the typical method of extending the lines of the house into the landscape. The central square of the terrace does not line up with the center of the pool, the bay window, or the corner of the house, which would have made the design simple. The terrace is free to anchor all these disparate elements. To come in through the garden gate and stand on axis would be boring.

That it is not predictable is proof of our close collaboration with the client, architect and interior designer—evidence which shows in every detail. The strong architecture of this house suggested many opportunities to carry architectural detail out into the garden, bringing unity and integrity to the design of the entire dwelling place.

Preceding page: The old brick wall has
been given a post-modern treatment of arches, half-
columns and arbor to gain a feeling of greater depth.
Atop the wall, *Clematis paniculata, Campsis radicans*
(trumpet vine) and *Wisteria* are coiling over a
wrought iron trellis designed to hide the
neighbor's unsightly air conditioning equipment.
Planting up to the pool coping includes
deep yellow *Ligularia dentata* 'Desdemona'
and *Nandina domestica* on the right. *Ilex* x *attenuata*
'Fosteri' stand in the corner, next to a delicate
pink *Hibiscus moscheutos*—the native hibiscus.
Calamagrostis acutiflora stricta creates the illusion of
the meadow even in this limited space.
Photograph by Valerie Brown.

True to the house's post-modern spirit, half-columns are applied to the existing garden wall. The columns "push" the wall back and seem to hold up the wooden arbor, creating the illusion of depth. A new, vine-covered wrought-iron trellis atop the wall screens the view. Its motif is an ornamented criss-cross which combines the terrace pattern with a medallion on the balcony railing. We espaliered *Pyracantha coccinea* (firethorn) on the wall by the poolhouse steps as a focal point to draw attention away from the gas grill. As the wall continues along the poolhouse, it makes a perfectly contained space for a fringe of *Phyllostachys aureosulcata* (yellow-groove bamboo) behind lattice, screening poolhouse windows and creating an enigmatic, soft view from the living room.

Above: Details require not only care in design and quality of materials, but craftsmanship in execution. The Schneiderman Garden is completely edged in limestone with an incised bead and canted top. Limestone stringers take their direction from the corner. The groundcover is *Ceratostigma plumbaginoides.*
Photograph by James van Sweden.

Opposite: Winter frosts the garden and pool. In the foreground is dried *Miscanthus sinensis purpurascens;* its delicate mauve look picks up the color of the redwood arbor. The trellis was designed in collaboration with the architects to reference the ironwork detail on the second story balcony.
Photograph by Valerie Brown.

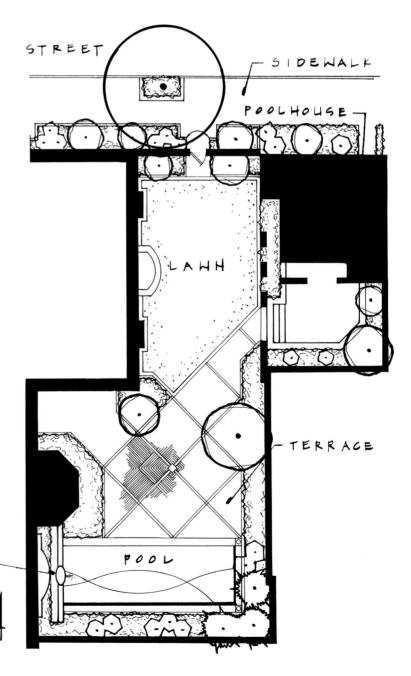

STREET

SIDEWALK

POOLHOUSE

LAWN

TERRACE

FOUNTAIN

POOL

0 5 10 20

Opposite: Designed as a false facade for the guest and pool house, brick arches and pediments with intricate latticework are backplanted with *Phyllostachys aureosulcata* (yellow-groove bamboo) and provide a focal point across the lawn from the living room. The "eyelid" of arbor is planted with *Lonicera periclymenum* (fragrant woodbine) to bloom in early summer. Intended for children's play, the carpet of lawn also extends the terrace for large parties. Photograph by Michael McKinley.

Mid-summer. Photograph by Michael McKinley.

PERENNIALS

- **a.** *Astilbe* x *arendsii* 'Red Sentinel'   (hybrid red false spirea)
- **b.** *Liriope muscari* 'Big Blue'
- **c.** *Helleborus orientalis*   (Lenten rose)
- **d.** *Ligularia dentata* 'Desdemona'
- **e.** *Brunnera macrophylla*
- **f.** *Aralia racemosa*

GRASSES

- **A.** *Miscanthus sinensis purpurascens*

TREES, SHRUBS & VINES

1. *Magnolia virginiana*
2. *Stewartia pseudocamellia*   (Japanese stewartia)
3. *Amelanchier canadensis*
4. *Fargesia nitida*
5. *Nandina domestica*
6. *Wisteria* sp.

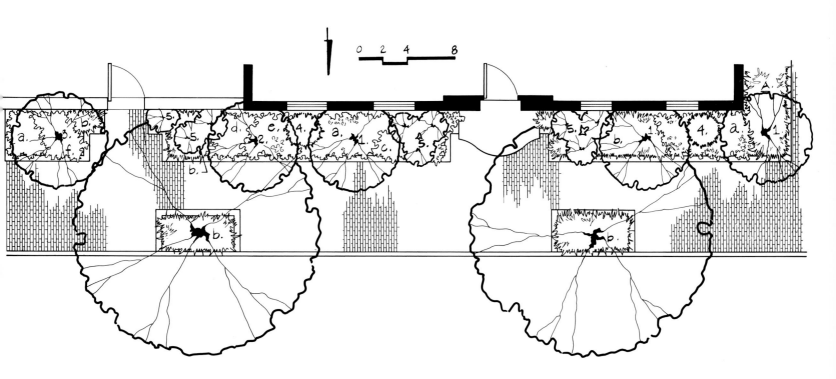

The carved limestone button marks the corner of the pool and the contrast between the feathery *Calamagrostis acutiflora stricta* and the bold foliage of *Hibiscus moscheutos.* Later in the summer the large blooms will shimmer on the dark water. *Ceratostigma plumbaginoides* spills over the limestone edge. Photograph by Peter Jones.

"We very much wanted the design to include a grassy area which has turned out to be a beautiful element of the garden. It is big enough for the girls to hula hoop on, and a fun place to have picnics."
—Karen Schneiderman

It is of prime importance to instill as much mystery and green sensation as possible in such a limited space. The sunken garden of the poolhouse plays that role here. From the living room, the view carries through a portal in the brick wall, down several steps, to give a feeling of space without end.

We pulled stringers of limestone from the base of the house across the floor of the garden, tying everything together. Bowed steps from the living room are coped in limestone, which continues around the lawn as does the coping around the swimming pool. Deeply carved circles of limestone at the pool corners repeat a button on the house above French doors. Limestone stringers in the terrace multiply the organizing diagonal to further exaggerate the sense of greater space. Designed as a square within a square within a square, the terrace is divided into quadrants. Within each quadrant, the brick changes direction for a quilted effect. Bricks laid on edge fool the eye into perceiving a greater size.

At Karen Schneiderman's suggestion, we included lawn as a soft place for the children to play. It also serves as a bordered carpet in the event of large parties. Planting is not dominant within the garden walls. Since the garden is small and quite formal, we used simple but interesting plants to loosen up the space. One bold sweep of *Calamagrostis acutiflora stricta* at the end of the pool terrace gives that semi-shady spot a textural "oomph" and relief from detail.

It is a different story outside, along the public sidewalk. When Milton Schneiderman asked that the house be screened, he inadvertently set a linear garden in motion. The four-foot wide border is as finely detailed with limestone edging as in the private garden, and the planting design never repeats. The garden strip unrolls in a progression of plants from one end of the house, around the corner, to the other end. Changing continually through the seasons, it has become a marvelous learning tool as passersby often inquire about the plants. The people of Georgetown love this border because the Schneidermans have given them such richness to enjoy from the sidewalk.

Detail of the pool house window with
Lonicera periclymenum trailing on the right, and
Phyllostachys aureosulcata underplanted
with *Lamiastrum galeobdolon* (yellow archangel).
Photograph by Peter Jones.

We opened up a solidly wooded lot to create a vista with light and space for the Anne Lloyd Garden in Washington, D.C. Forty-two bluestone steps lead down from the house to a terrace along a stream which we dammed to make two ponds. Designed for an active family with little boys, the ponds have a concrete and stone floor so that they can be cleaned easily.

The stream terrace is actually in the front yard, so a large number of *Ilex* x *attenuata* 'Nellie R. Stevens' were planted around the perimeter to screen the street. The native woodland is a mixture of *Sassafras albidum* and *Fagus grandifolia* (American beech), with a very old *Liriodendron tulipifera* (tulip tree) on the near left side of the photograph. In the foreground are shade garden plantings, including *Podophyllum peltatum* (Mayapple), *Trillium grandiflorum* (white wake-robin), *Sanguinaria canadensis* (bloodroot), a collection of ferns, and a mass of *Lamiastrum galeobdolon* (yellow archangel). *Hedera* (ivy) cascades downhill toward mounds of young *Skimmia japonica* at the bottom of the stairs. Photograph by John Neubauer.

W hen the Rosenbergs found their weekend house on brackish Mecox Bay behind the South Shore dunes, they wanted a garden that would respond to its wide-open setting. But the site imposes rough growing conditions of wind, salt air and poor-quality fill dirt, and the leisure of a home away from home called for limited maintenance. Artist Buffy Johnson had already designed the swimming pool by the time we came on the scene. Its curvilinear form echoes the simple sweep of the inlet, but the pool and terraces did not flow together within the larger landscape. The Rosenbergs are gregarious hosts, so the garden needed to accommodate any number of people from one to one hundred.

The design takes off on its larger, borrowed landscape of water and sky, simply joined with a sweeping line of marsh. As a horizontal garden that grows to predictable size every year, it will never hide the view. Three clumps of *Miscanthus floridulus* are triangulated in the lawn, providing a strong focal point. Standing against a panoramic background of *Phragmites australis* (common reed), the tall *M. floridulus* link the new with the native above a continuous plane of water and turf.

A deep midzone border of grasses and perennials mediates between the outer landscape and inner garden areas. Piercing the border, three walkways lead to a vegetable garden, formal terrace and pool terrace. Paving alongside the house links all three areas.

Opposite: In early summer, the border of the Rosenberg Garden on Long Island, is framed by *Magnolia virginiana* (left), and by the variegated *Miscanthus sinensis strictus* (right), above layers of *Lavandula angustifolia* 'Hidcote' (English lavender), *Perovskia atriplicifolia* and *Helictotrichon sempervirens*. (Photograph by Michael McKinley.) Above: In the driveway's oval planting island, are a sea of *Sedum* x *telephium* 'Autumn Joy' and sprays of *Pennisetum alopecuroides* in front of a mound of *Panicum virgatum*. Photograph by Ken Druse.

Horizontal layers meld the Rosenberg Garden to its natural landscape of marsh and bay, exploiting the "genius of the place" with a sweeping curve of perennials and grasses including *Achillea filipendulina* 'Parker's Variety' under the existing *Salix babylonica* (weeping willow), *Miscanthus sinensis condensatus* to the right, and in the distance, the existing wetland *Phragmites australis* (common reed). Photograph by Ken Druse.

Preceding page: In the stillness of winter, peering through the *Molinia arundinacea* 'Windspiel' across the covered swimming pool at the soft brushes of *Pennisetum alopecuroides* and frothy plumes of *Miscanthus sinensis gracillimus*. Photograph by Marina Schinz.

Mid-summer. Photograph by James van Sweden.

PERENNIALS

a. *Achillea filipendulina*

b. *Sedum* x 'Ruby Glow'

c. *Perovskia atriplicifolia*

d. *Lavandula angustifolia* 'Hidcote'   (English lavender)

e. *Hemerocallis* sp.   (daylily)

f. *Lythrum salicaria* 'Morden's Pink'

GRASSES & SEDGES

A. *Panicum virgatum* 'Haense Herms'

B. *Pennisetum alopecuroides*

C. *Helictotrichon sempervirens*

D. *Molinia arundinacea* 'Windspiel'   (tall purple moor grass)

E. *Miscanthus sinensis strictus*   (porcupine grass)

F. *Festuca mairei*   (fescue)

G. *Miscanthus sinensis condensatus*   (purple-blooming Japanese silver grass)

H. *Elymus glaucus*   (blue wild rye)

I. *Miscanthus sinensis gracillimus*

J. *Spodiopogon sibiricus*

K. *Phragmites australis*   (common reed)

TREES & SHRUBS

1. *Salix babylonica*   (weeping willow)

2. *Ilex crenata convexa*   (Japanese holly)

3. *Magnolia virginiana*

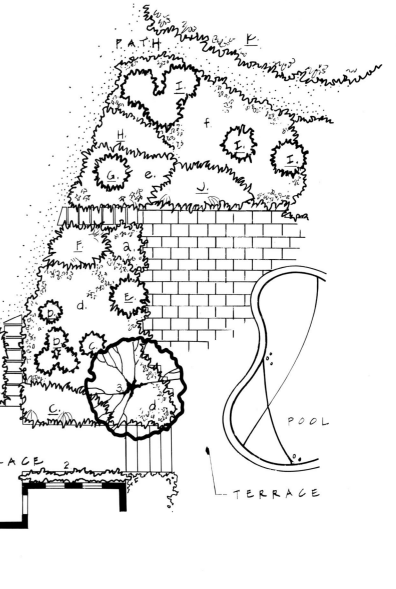

The view from the pool terrace evolves dramatically over three seasons. Late spring features *Lavandula angustifolia* 'Hidcote' in purple bloom with *Perovskia atriciplifolia* just beginning to emerge. The globes of *Allium giganteum* (ornamental onion) seem to float in the inflorescence of *Molinia arundinaceae* 'Windspiel', and in the *Miscanthus sinensis condensatus* beyond. (Photograph by Michael McKinley.) Autumn finds the foreground *Helictotrichon sempervirens* bleaching out. The parade of autumn glories marching along the lawn, from left, begins with *Molinia arundinaceae* 'Windspiel', *Panicum virgatum* 'Haense Herms', and *Pennisetum alopecuroides,* concluded by *Miscanthus sinensis condensatus.* (Photograph by Peter Jones.) Winter's spare and bony look features *Miscanthus sinensis gracillimus* in the foreground, with *Pennisetum alopecuroides* at the center, and rabbit tracks in the snow. Photograph by Ken Druse.

Above: Fenced with turkey wire, the vegetable, herb and cut flower beds are reached through a border of *Perovskia atriplicifolia* with *Sedum* x 'Ruby Glow' and *Achillea filipendulina* 'Parker's Variety' under the *Salix babylonica. Opposite:* In the swimming pool "world," planting is brought to the edge of the water for reflections and a more natural look. Mid-summer finds two tiers of ornamental grasses overhanging the pool—*Pennisetum alopecuroides* in front of *Miscanthus sinensis gracillimus;* to their left, stands the light green foliage of *Inula magnifica* (elecampane) bearing yellow flowers while *Hemerocallis* hybrids repeat the clear hues. Photographs by James van Sweden.

The formal terrace, right outside the living room, is most directly related to the water. The view is simply framed by a "balustrade" of *Pennisetum alopecuroides* which is woven into the more varied border at either end. Broad new steps connect the existing, formal terrace to the pool terrace and manage the change in grade, while the border glides uninterrupted from level to level.

Around the pool, the planting design is at its most complex. This is where people are most likely to relax and notice subtle detail. Although the pool terrace is just a few steps away from the parking bay and auto court, it is well buffered by a bordered walkway and several trees.

Out front, a bold design celebrates arrival to this retreat from Manhattan. Here we arranged structural plants on a mounded oval island centered in the auto court. In the background, a simple line of *Pinus thunbergiana* (Japanese black pine) plays against the driveway and screens neighboring houses.

Trees are otherwise scantly used here, out of respect for the site's essential quality of open space. One *Salix babylonica* 'Pendula' (weeping willow) marks the entrance to the vegetable and cut flower garden, located on the protected north side of the property. Turkey wire in plain wooden frames keeps the rabbits out of three beds for vegetables, herbs and cut flowers. Together the beds form a tight geometric block centered on the house, making the strongest architectural statement of a very informal garden.

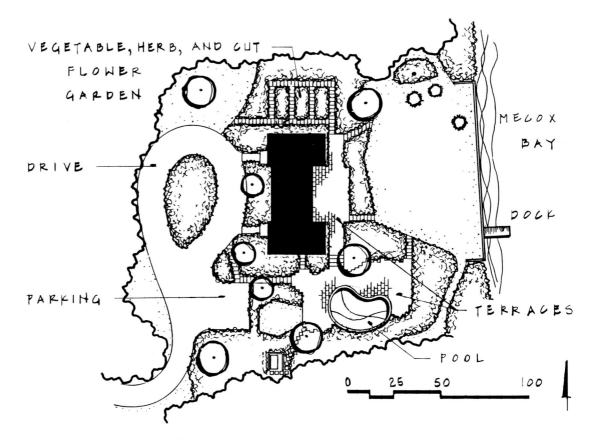

VEGETABLE, HERB, AND CUT FLOWER GARDEN

DRIVE

PARKING

MECOX BAY

DOCK

TERRACES

POOL

0   25   50   100

"We wanted to create a landscape that looked as
though it was always there. Ornamental
grasses add beautiful plumes and sounds to the
natural reeds along the water as they move with the
constant breeze off the Bay. Some grasses stand
like sculpture, while others soften hard
edges. Their textures and colors weave
incredible patterns."
— Carole Rosenberg

In Naples, Florida, two gardens show how our basic design principles extend to a different palette of plants. Opposite: The "New American Front Yard" is a showcase garden for the sales office of the Pelican Bay residential development. Like sculpture, existing *Pinus elliottii* (slash pine) trees stud the meadow of *Wedelia trilobata*. Dense planting screens the front walk to the house's double red doors. Leading from the driveway at left is the *Zamia floridana* (coontie), with the grayed foliage of *Nerium oleander* (common oleander) next to it at the center of the photograph. On the far right stands an existing *Sabal palmetto* (American palmetto).

Looking at the Turner Garden (left), from the second floor, the pool terrace is decked with bleached cypress and enfolded with bold mass plantings and sculptural forms coming up out of the thickly covered ground plane. The hot pink of *Lagerstroemia indica* (crape myrtle) contrasts with the cool blue-gray foliage of *Conocarpus erectus sericeus* (silver buttonwood). Photographs by Michael McKinley.

JAPAN INSPIRES A SIDE GARDEN

The Platt Garden

The truly serendipitous project finds the site, the client and the designers in absolute agreement. Having recently returned from a study trip in Japan, we undertook the design of a new garden for Ambassador and Mrs. Platt, who had lived in and admired Japan very much. The Platts did not request a Japanese garden, nor did we wish to design one, yet this garden in a Western idiom has clear sympathies with Japan. The interpenetration of house and garden is complete; and certain material details, such as the wood and stucco wall and stepping stones, recall a Japanese sensibility. Yet spaces in the garden are put together to suit Western family and social patterns, and the planting palette is international.

Tucked behind several *Taxus cuspidata* (Japanese yew) and an iron gate, the house is approached by a narrow brick walk which has been relaid and dressed up with planting. Entering the house is almost like stepping into the garden, which immediately presents itself through large windows from the living and dining rooms.

Although a small garden, its two levels and L-shape create a variety of views and spaces. From the dining room's slate floor, you walk directly out onto a large bluestone terrace sized for entertaining. Three stones set on the diagonal climb to the upper level, where plantings predominate and brush against the walls. Flat stones wander through the garden to a second, more intimate terrace often used for breakfast. A few more stepping stones turn left toward a secluded alcove for a bench where children like to play. The brick wall overflows with *Hedera helix* (English ivy). Seen at eye level when seated in the kitchen-family room, the upper garden seems to flow back into the house.

Opposite: Night lighting extends the Platts' home outside into the garden. The view from the living room takes in all the effects: washes on the back walls to silhouette plants; uplights into tree canopies; spotlights on seasonal interests; path lights; and a flood-wash mounted on the house to light the terrace. *Above:* A very simple terrace at the back of the garden is a favorite place for family breakfasts. In the foreground, stepping stones lead to a bench niche in the "L" of this tiny town garden. Photographs by Michael McKinley.

Early summer. Photograph by Michael McKinley.

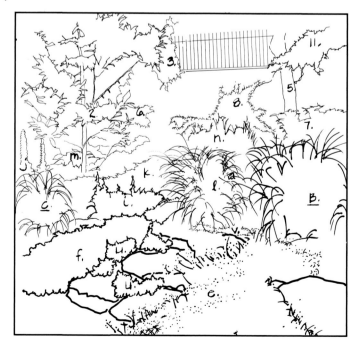

PERENNIALS

a. *Liriope muscari* 'Big Blue'

b. *Astilbe taquetii* 'Superba' (purple rose false spirea)

c. *Brunnera macrophylla*

d. *Hypericum calycinum* 'Hidcote' (St.-John's-wort)

e. *Coreopsis verticillata* 'Moonbeam'

f. *Heuchera sanguinea* 'Bressingham Hybrids' (coralbells)

g. *Perovskia atriplicifolia*

h. *Agapanthus umbellatus* 'Blue Triumphator' (lily-of-the-Nile)

i. *Stachys byzantina* (lamb's-ears)

j. *Acanthus hungaricus*

k. *Ceratostigma plumbaginoides*

l. *Hemerocallis liliaceae* 'Stella d'Oro'

m. *Begonia grandis*

n. *Iris kaempferi* (Japanese iris) and *I. sibirica* (Siberian iris)

o. *Hosta* x 'Royal Standard' (plantain lily)

p. *H.* x 'Honeybells' (plantain lily)

q. *Ligularia dentata* 'Desdemona'

r. *Helleborus orientalis* (Lenten rose)

s. *Athyrium filix-femina* (lady fern) with *Anemone hupehensis japonica* 'September Charm' (Japanese anemone)

t. *Astilbe* x *arendsii* 'Diamant' (hybrid white false spirea)

u. *Sedum* x 'Ruby Glow'

v. *Thymus pseudolanuginosus* (creeping thyme)

GRASSES & SEDGES

A. *Molinia arundinacea* 'Windspiel' (tall purple moor grass)

B. *Miscanthus sinensis purpurascens*

C. *Pennisetum alopecuroides*

TREES, SHRUBS & VINES

1. *Zelkova serrata*

2. *Magnolia virginiana*

3. *M. grandiflora* (southern magnolia)

4. *Ilex* x *attenuata* 'Fosteri'

5. *Malus* sp. (flowering crabapple)

6. *Nandina domestica*

7. *Kalmia latifolia* (mountain laurel)

8. *Fargesia nitida*

9. *Pieris japonica* (lily-of-the-valley bush)

10. *Rhododendron* sp. (azalea)

11. *Wisteria* sp.

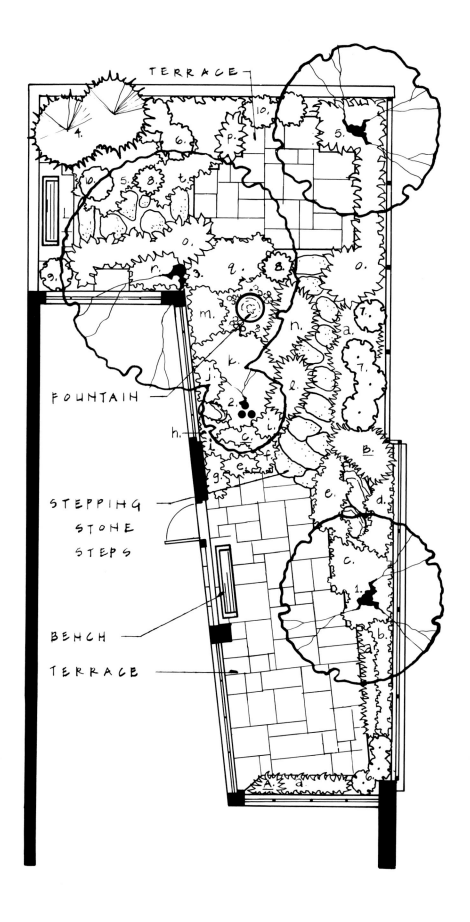

Right: Seated on the family room sofa, you can look at eye level into an intimate view of the fountain and visiting birds, and *Fargesia nitida* framed by the Japanese-inspired fence of redwood with a rank of louvers stretched across the top.
Opposite: Moving water creates a quiet zone in the rear garden. Reminiscent of a millstone, the limestone fountain is carved with a quarter-inch lip to hold water as it bubbles up through a center hole, smoothly moves across to the edge, and falls to the stones below. The fountain "floats" (on a stuccoed brick support) above riverwashed stones that cover a steel grate and concrete basin—the reservoir for the recirculating fountain. Surrounding plantings, especially *Iris kaempferi* (Japanese iris), traditionally are associated with water, and the fountain's trickling sound and cooling effect attracts many birds, creating both a visual and an auditory focal point. Photographs by Michael McKinley.

With such strong interconnections, the garden walls and fence take on the important role of reinforcing the sequence of garden areas. Brick walls to the north and east wrap around the alcove and upper terrace, whereas the south fence is a stylized backdrop uniting the lower and upper levels. Inspired by a temple wall seen on the Japanese trip, we stuccoed a fragment of old garage foundations and topped it with a detailed redwood fence, which continues along the length of the upper garden.

As a whole, the garden pivots on a simple fountain at the visual intersection of all three spaces. We modeled it after a millstone, with a center bubbler and a very shallow lip. The rippling water, as it moves toward the edge and over the sides, is a magnet for birds. They flock there in constant motion and are beautiful to see at eye-level from the kitchen-family room, like a periscope view across the water's surface.

"Coming home from working abroad, often in tropical countries, we move back into our house and garden with particular delight in the seasons. Sometimes we catch the first daffodils, sometimes the amazing crabapple blooms with mountain laurel following, or maybe the garden is winter green and white with snow on the holly and nandina."
—Sheila and Nicholas Platt

Surrounding a pool terrace on a country hillside,
the Offutts' garden relates to the wider
landscape of pasture and farmland. *Opposite:*
Calamagrostis acutiflora stricta is planted
like a balustrade along the horizon end of the terrace,
defining the edge of the designed garden.
(Photograph by Michael McKinley.) *Above:* Like
a ha-ha wall, a mass of *Achillea filipendulina* 'Parker's
Variety' almost makes the pasture fence disappear.
Photograph by James van Sweden.

*I*t is hard to imagine a more perfect country setting than this quiet knoll north of Baltimore. Yet the pastoral landscape of hill and valley was almost too commanding, and the view from the house was dominated by a distant cluster of farm buildings. The Offutts had tried to block out the farm by planting large evergreens at the property line. They merely discovered a lackluster foreground, and wondered if a new swimming pool might rescue the situation.

We immediately saw that this was the wrong place for a pool, as it would create a forlorn winter view from the living room. Instead, we extended and regraded the level lawn to be cupped by gentle slopes on either side. With selective pruning of the evergreen screen, this area's breadth now gives a sense of unimpeded views. Ornamental planting distinguishes the slopes and eases transitions up to terraces on either end of the house.

Nestled on the southwest just beyond the driveway service court is an existing entry terrace, newly framed by *Calamagrostis acutiflora stricta, Pennisetum alopecuroides* and *Acanthus hungaricus.* Coming down existing steps around the side of the house, you look across the lawn to perennial borders. Through these wide borders, three steps lead diagonally up to the new pool terrace at the northeast end of the house.

Late summer. Photograph by Michael McKinley.

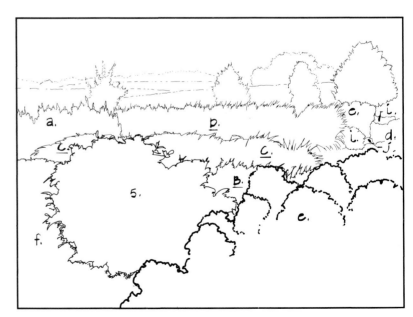

PERENNIALS

a. *Lythrum salicaria* 'Morden's Pink'

b. *Acanthus hungaricus*

c. *Ceratostigma plumbaginoides*

d. *Achillea filipendulina*

e. *Eupatorium purpureum* 'Gateway'

f. *Rudbeckia fulgida* 'Goldsturm'

g. *Yucca filamentosa*

h. *Hemerocallis* sp.   (daylily)

i. *Sedum* x *telephium* 'Autumn Joy'

j. *Coreopsis verticillata* 'Moonbeam'

GRASSES & SEDGES

A. *Panicum virgatum* 'Haense Herms'

B. *Pennisetum orientale*   (orient fountain grass)

C. *P. alopecuroides*

D. *Calamagrostis acutiflora stricta*

E. *Miscanthus sinensis gracillimus*

TREES & SHRUBS

1. *Crataegus phaenopyrum*   (Washington hawthorn)

2. *Aralia spinosa*   (Devil's-walking stick)

3. *Viburnum setigerum*   (tea viburnum)

4. *V. rhytidophyllum*   (leatherleaf viburnum)

5. *V.* x *pragense*

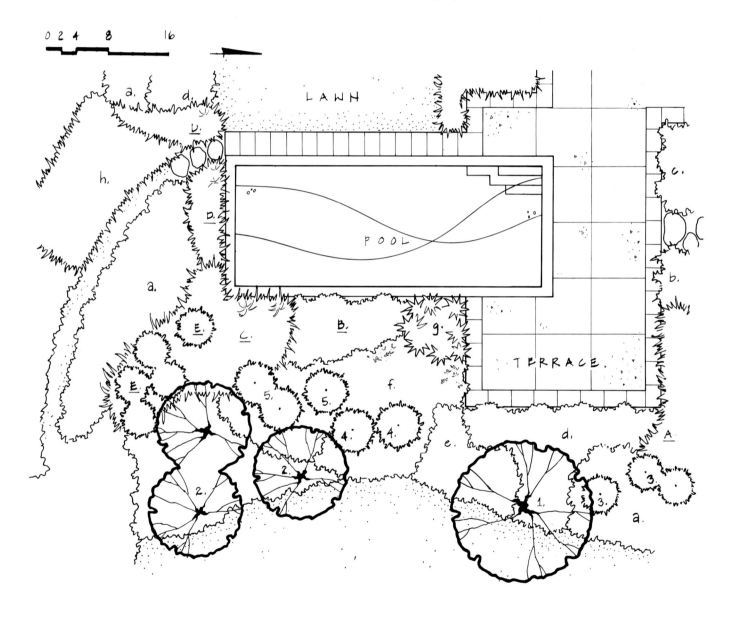

Right: From the entrance court, stairs at the corner of the house lead down to the lawn, which then sweeps up to the pool terrace. The transition of lawn to pasture is blurred by a long border. Morning light catches the new inflorescence of *Pennisetum alopecuroides.*
Left: Green as malachite, the lawn swirls through the metaphorical meadow to the pasture beyond like a seamless carpet. The stripes of autumn color, from front to back: *Panicum virgatum* 'Haense Herms', *Rudbeckia fulgida* 'Goldsturm', *Pennisetum alopecuroides, Sedum* x *telephium* 'Autumn Joy' and *Calamagrostis acutiflora stricta.* Dried seedheads of *Astilbe* underplant an old flowering *Prunus* (cherry). Photographs by Michael McKinley.

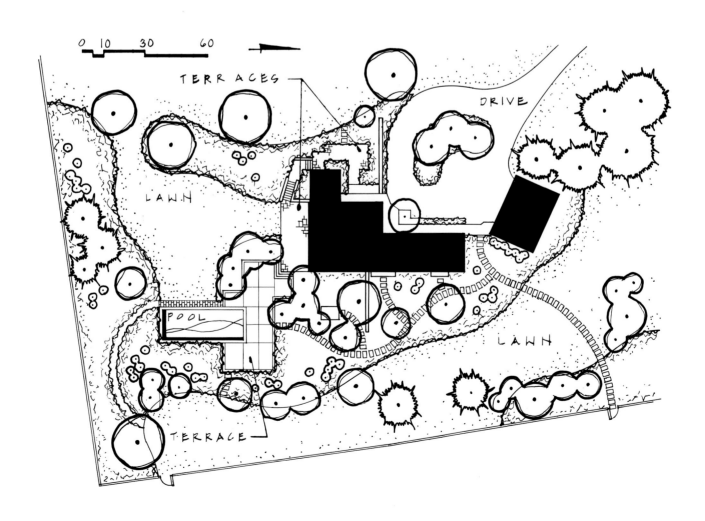

Setting the pool terrace into the slope at midpoint between the lower lawn and upper meadow protects swimmers from the wind, extending the pool season into cooler months. This elevation fully claims the farm view, while effectively screening it from the house. From the pool, a rusticated series of steps and landings trail up the slope toward horse stables.

Washed aggregate concrete is suitably casual at poolside. Its coarse texture safeguards against slippage, and the reflectivity of its light color makes for a cool surface underfoot. We used the same gravel as in the aggregate paving to mulch the plantings for a subtle contrast. Bluestone edging separates mulch from paving and ties the new landscape to the existing bluestone terrace.

Fencing in a simple vernacular style defines the edge of the property, before the land slips quickly downslope in a profusion of *Hemerocallis* species. Like a "ha-ha" (unseen retaining wall for livestock control), this edge virtually eliminates a middleground view. Planting the foreground to such a dramatic background requires the strength of simplicity. Huge meadow-drifts of color match the scale of the outer landscape, visually drawing together a total garden world. The plant masses read as stacked horizontal layers, almost a foundation planting, in support of the far horizon.

Sometimes, as a garden grows, its owners grow into gardeners. Nelson and Karen Offutt have embarked on such a path of increasing involvement, from caring for the plants to studying at Longwood Gardens.[9]

"Chip and I enjoy spending many hours in the garden. Home is so much more enjoyable that it is difficult to leave at any time of the year, but especially between May and October when the grasses and perennials are at their peak. We started out with a basically beautiful landscape and wound up with a great work of art. I call it my 'Chagall wall'."
—Karen Offutt

A garden for Maija Hay's potting studio in Washington, D.C. is programmed as an exhibition space as well as for the enjoyment of her students. Thus, the terrace and bench are designed for the display of pots and the indoor potting studio overlooks a large lily pond. To give the flat garden some vertical dimension, the central planting bed is lightly mounded and planted with *Yucca filamentosa* and *Inula magnifica* (elecampane). The giant blooms of *Heracleum mantegazzianum* (giant hogweed) frame the lower edge of this view from the second floor balcony off the master bedroom; at right is an *Aralia spinosa* (Devil's-walking stick). Photograph by Michael McKinley.

LILY POOL IN THE BACKYARD

The Littlefield Garden

Changing levels enlarge the small flat space behind the Littlefields' Victorian home. Lifting the L-shaped lily pool up to bench height also creates seating that wraps around the bluestone terrace for large parties. The fountain jet is placed on axis with the front door to magnify the connection between house and garden, and thus the total living space. Looking through French doors from the dining room gives a sense of the compelling view that greets you upon entering the house. In spring, lily-flowering *Tulipa* hybrids predominate, complemented by pots of *Lantana montevidensis* (lantana) and *Agapanthus umbellatus* 'Blue Triumphator' (lily-of-the-Nile) planted by Dr. Littlefield. Photograph by John Neubauer.

An anachronism on one of America's great streets of Federal houses, this ordinary frame house was built during the opening years of the automobile age, much to the garden's detriment. A three-stall garage stretched across the entire backyard. Concrete covered the ground, painted green to simulate grass.

A three-stall garage is very valuable to most city dwellers, but Dr. and Mrs. Littlefield saw that removing the garage was the only way to have a house-and-garden. By simply placing the car next to the house and as close to the street as possible, the back garden gains all the space taken up by the driveway and garage.

Now you enter through a gate in the fence, following stepping stones through planting to the main garden. It is evenly allocated to a bluestone terrace and an L-shaped lily pool raised to bench height to alleviate the garden's flatness. We used soil won from digging the pool to sculpt the planting bed at the back of the garden. At eighteen inches above terrace level, the raised bed gives extra height to the *Ilex* x *attenuata* 'Fosteri', *Tsuga canadensis* (Canadian hemlock) and *Miscanthus floridulus* for adequately screening the neighbors. We extended the pool walls to lengthen the bench, tying the garden together and articulating the terrace edge. People enjoy sitting right at the pool's edge, dangling their hands in the water, close to the fish and the bubbling fountain. The entire scene becomes one when the new dining and sitting room are open to the terrace; from above, a balcony from the master bedroom looks down on the garden as into a jewel box.

An ophthalmologist, Jerald Littlefield works in the dark all day, so he loves being outside. Active gardening is his great relief. He is the perfect client for a lily pool because he enjoys giving it all the attention it requires. But for a little bit of work, lily pools offer a never-ending fascination, giving a huge return on the energy invested.

Mid-summer. Photograph by John Neubauer.

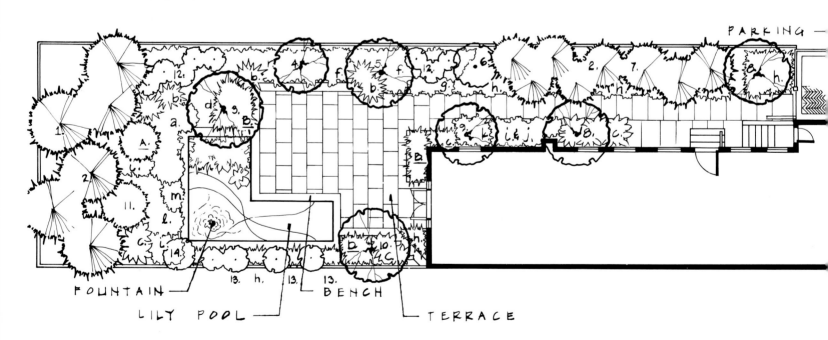

PERENNIALS

a. *Rudbeckia fulgida* 'Goldsturm'

b. *Yucca filamentosa*

c. *Hosta sieboldiana*

d. *Anemone hupehensis japonica* 'September Charm' (Japanese anemone)

e. *Aralia racemosa*

f. *Brunnera macrophylla*

g. *Acanthus hungaricus*

h. *Liriope muscari* 'Big Blue'

i. *Ligularia dentata* 'Desdemona'

j. *Helleborus orientalis* (Lenten rose)

k. *Epimedium* x *versicolor* (long-spur epimedium)

l. *Dennstaedtia punctilobula* (hay-scented-fern)

m. *Galium odoratum* (sweet woodruff)

n. *Columnea* x *banksii* (columnea)

o. *Typha angustifolia* (narrow-leaved cattail)

p. *Pontederia cordata* (pickerelweed)

q. *Impatiens* sp. (touch-me-not)

r. *Hibiscus moscheutos*

s. *Nelumbo nucifera* (sacred lotus)

t. *Agapanthus umbellatus* 'Blue Triumphator' (lily-of-the-Nile)

GRASSES & SEDGES

A. *Miscanthus sinensis gracillimus*

B. *Pennisetum alopecuroides*

C. *Calamagrostis acutiflora stricta*

D. *Carex pendula*

TREES & SHRUBS

1. *Tsuga canadensis* (Canadian hemlock)

2. *Ilex* x *attenuata* 'Fosteri'

3. *Styrax japonica* (Japanese snowbell)

4. *Photinia* x *fraseri* (Fraser photinia)

5. *Cornus kousa*

6. *Hamamelis* x *intermedia* 'Arnold Promise'

7. *Ilex* x 'Nellie R. Stevens'

8. *Aralia spinosa* (Devil's-walking stick)

9. *Amelanchier canadensis*

10. *Magnolia virginiana*

11. *Fargesia nitida*

12. *Nandina domestica*

13. *Mahonia bealei*

14. *Skimmia japonica* (Japanese skimmia)

15. *Magnolia grandiflora* (southern magnolia)

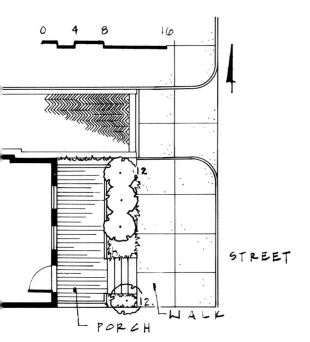

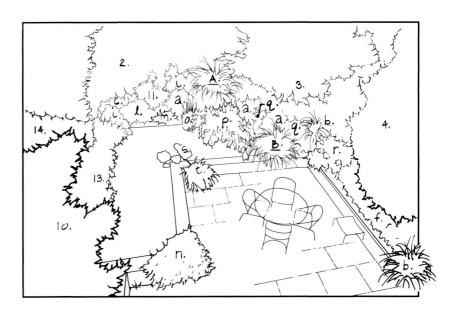

Right: The fountain is left on all winter so that ice forms and reforms around it. Rising as much as five feet high, the jet is controlled by a rheostat inside the house. The pool is framed on the left by the dried seedheads of the *Miscanthus sinensis gracillimus* and overhead by the neighbor's *Magnolia grandiflora* (southern magnolia). *Opposite:* Following the garden design, a dining room and upstairs master suite were added to open the house on both levels to the garden, taking in the views and extending living space outdoors. A *Magnolia virginiana* frames the dining room arch on the right, with *Mahonia bealei* planted the length of the lily pool along the stockade fence. In mid-summer the yellow *Rudbeckia fulgida* 'Goldsturm' begins to bloom, framing a water-based planting of *Sagittaria latifolia* (arrowhead) and *Typha angustifolia* (narrow-leaf cattail). To the left of the house is the pathway to the streetside gate and parking. Photographs by John Neubauer.

"The 'Littlefield priority' is to make a garden first and build the house around it. When choosing a new home, we look for a good garden space that is easily accessible from indoor living areas. The garden is our playroom; maintaining its eternal beauty is my leisure."
—Jerald Littlefield

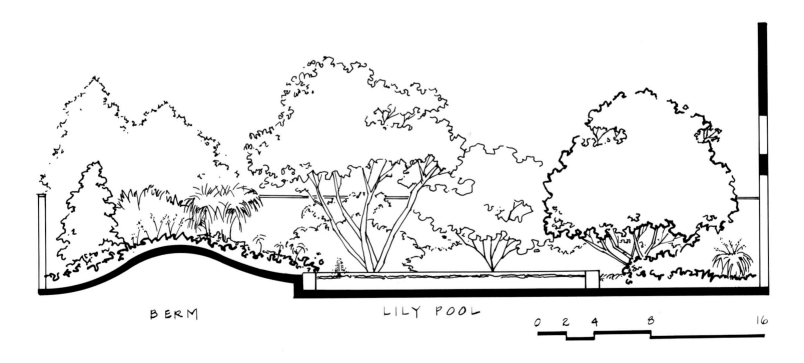

BERM   LILY POOL   0 2 4   8   16

EMBRACING THE SUBURBAN HOME

The Gratz Garden

A n American prototype, this property is a classic example of early suburban land use, dating from 1905. The large, shingled bungalow house sits in the middle of a quarter-acre lot; behind a fence, an alley services the garage.

This is a soft garden, with little construction and a very simple hardscape of bluestone pavers. Since Jacqueline Gratz is a consummate gardener, the plant list is lavish. There is no borrowed scenery. The entire view was created with the help of some mature trees and beautiful *Hydrangea paniculata* 'Grandiflora' (peegee hydrangea) which effectively screen neighboring houses.

The front gate opens upon several old *Picea pungens glauca* (Colorado blue spruce) which are strangely sculptural. It is like walking through a sliver of forest before coming into the garden. To the right is a layer of planting which screens the front garden. Straight ahead at the front porch, a broad border of grasses, *Molinia arundinacea* 'Windspiel' (purple moor grass) and *Miscanthus sinensis condensatus* (Japanese silver grass) reaches above the balustrade. It forms a loose screen without blocking the view, and gives privacy from the public street. In the center of the front garden, a small lawn sets off the perennial planting. Walking across the lawn, you pick up a paved path which meanders through lush planting along the south side of the house to the back.

Well-suited to a typical American house,
the Gratzes' free-spirited garden is all about plants.
Opposite: The base of the house is softened
by a palette of yellow-blooming *Telekia speciosa,*
Astilbe species' red and pink spikes, and a branch of
Picea pungens glauca (Colorado blue spruce).
(Photograph by Michael McKinley.)
Above: Cytisus x *praecox* (Warminster broom)
is a fountain of pale yellow at the at the porch's edge.
Photograph by Michael Selig.

Right: The summer border features a dramatic clump of cool-yellow *Verbascum olympicum* (mullein), in contrast to the hot yellow of *Rudbeckia fulgida* 'Goldsturm' in the foreground. *Below right:* Screened on the left by a *Macleaya cordata* underplanted with *Pachysandra terminalis* (Japanese pachysandra), an enticing view through the alley gate welcomes the Gratzes home. Photographs by Michael McKinley.

Opposite: From the front porch, the view is through a delicate curtain of *Molinia arundinaceae* 'Windspiel', to the plumage of *Miscanthus sinensis gracillimus*. The street and sidewalk are fully screened. Photograph by Valerie Brown.

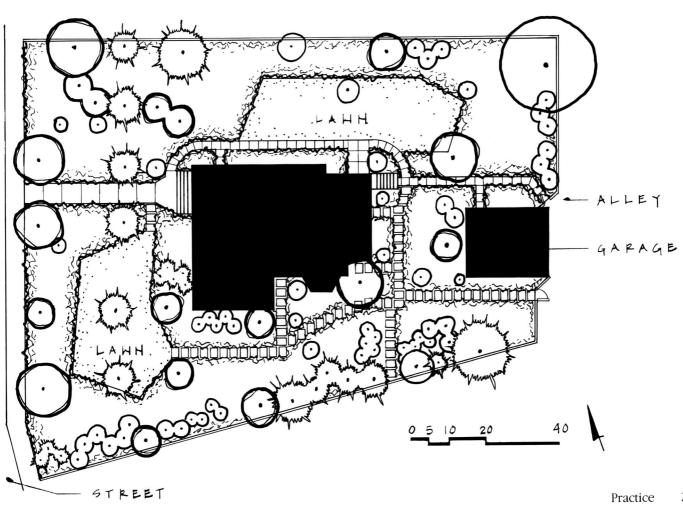

LAHH

LAHH

ALLEY

GARAGE

0 5 10   20   40

STREET

Early summer. Photograph by Michael McKinley.

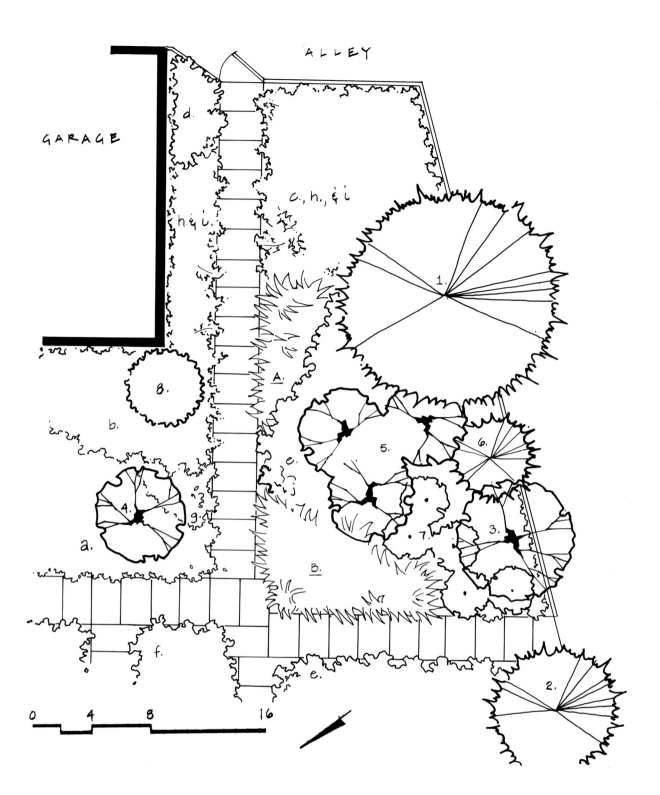

ALLEY

GARAGE

PERENNIALS

a. *Epimedium niveum*   (white long-spur epimedium)

b. *Astilbe* x *arendsii*   (hybrid false spirea)

c. *Polystichum acrostichoides*   (Christmas fern)

d. *Aronia arbutifolia*   (chokeberry)

e. *Ligularia dentata* 'Desdemona'

f. *Brunnera macrophylla*

g. *Epimedium* x *rubrum*   (pink epimedium)

h. *Dennstaedtia punctilobula*   (hay-scented fern)

i. *Matteuccia pensylvanica*   (ostrich fern)

GRASSES & SEDGES

A. *Carex pendula*

B. *C. muskingumensis*   (palm sedge)

TREES & SHRUBS

1. *Tsuga canadensis*   (Canadian hemlock)

2. *Picea pungens glauca*   (Colorado blue spruce)

3. *Cercis canadensis*   (redbud)

4. *Viburnum setigerum*   (tea viburnum)

5. *Lindera benzoin*   (spicebush)

6. *Juniperus communis*   (common juniper)

7. *Photinia* x *fraseri*   (Fraser photinia)

8. *Fargesia nitida*

Opposite: An archetypal American back yard, with shaded lawn, comfortable chaises, and venerable plants like a *Hydrangea paniculata* 'Grandiflora' (peegee hydrangea). In the center of the lawn, is an umbrella of *Aralia spinosa* (Devil's walking-stick), while the lacy racemes of *Polygonum aubertii* drape the alley fence. Photograph by John Neubauer.

Overleaf: Here is an alternative to the old-fashioned "foundation planting," which is to design the garden as continuous planting from property line to facade. At right, the regal mauve flower stalks of *Acanthus hungaricus* complement the brown shingles, while *Molinia arundinacea* 'Windspiel' is a delicate architectural contrast. A sweep of *Liriope spicata* (creeping lily turf) edges the right side of the walk; in the left foreground is *Hypericum calycinum* (St.-John's-wort) with *Perovskia atriplicifolia* above. Along the bend of the path, the pink spires of *Astilbe chinensis pumila* (false spirea) are set off by the creamy inflorescence of *Pennisetum orientale* (oriental fountain grass). Photograph by Volkmar Wentzel.

"The garden gives so much in return for so little work. We used to travel miles away to feel in touch with the pulse of nature; now all I have to do is walk in my garden."
—Jacqueline Gratz

The circuit around the house is intersected by a walkway connecting the back door to the private service entrance from the alley. A small vegetable garden at the back fence is an attractive part of the view from a second panel of lawn. This green terrace acts as the garden's family room to the front lawn's formal parlor.

The walk continues on its way around the north side of the house, again between lawn and sumptuous planting. The bungalow is set high on a massive foundation which typically would be masked by dull evergreens, eventually getting out of hand and covering up the windows. We selected plants that grow to a predictable size each year, instead of needing to be pruned into an artificial shape. Matching the right perennials to the architecture gives a natural base that never grows larger than desired.

These plants, moreover, are not just piled against the foundations. They are part of the overall plan, the total picture, from the walls of the house to the edges of the property. Of course, the foundation shows during the brief hiatus from late winter to early spring, when the garden's dried bouquets are cut down. But even that bareness is interesting when the foundation has been painted a neutral shade and evergreen plants come into their own. A house has great visual strength when it comes right down to the ground.

As the year unfolds and the garden grows into summer, the foundation slowly disappears. Once more the house seems to float in a meadow.

Part III

Building

Elements of Architecture

A design concept comes to life through the complementary elements of building and planting. Both bring unity to the garden in visual and functional ways. Typically, built elements are designed before the plantings, as the "bones" of the design support the "flesh." While built elements are a powerful way to achieve dramatic unity in the garden's layout, it is important to execute them with a light touch. Otherwise the built elements can easily overpower the changing garden. Sculpting the earth, selecting materials, lining up details and meeting corners, treating edges, creating water features—all contrive to carry out the genius of the place.

Preceding page: In the Anne Lloyd Garden, an L-shaped pool has its center jet on axis with the library's French doors. The stone "lily pad" is set on a pedestal of concrete to provide the illusion of floating. Photograph by Jerry Harpur.

One kind of unity comes to the garden through its built elements. *Opposite:* At the Shockey Garden, white stucco walls carry out the architecture of the house, as a wooden bench mediates the woodland edge. Photograph by Michael McKinley.

TYING IT ALL TOGETHER

Materials must suit the situation. We take our cues from the vernacular context and the specific architecture of the building, as well as the budget. Usually, it is a matter of selecting construction materials that are indigenous to a region and treating them according to local traditions. Often what works in one region is absolutely wrong elsewhere. For example, coralstone is appropriate in Florida, yet its beautiful pitted texture prohibits use in the north because of freezing and thawing. Limestone suits the Midwest where it is quarried, just as bluestone belongs to the Mid-Atlantic region.

Contrast and exotica can also be desirable. In a way, there is more freedom to use new ideas and materials in the city, where there is often no visible tie to the regional landscape. To evoke a remembrance of Japan in the Platt's Georgetown garden, stucco, highly crafted redwood, and personable stones are important. At the contemporary Shockey residence, concrete is a pristine domestic presence in the Virginia woods. At the ocean, where informality prevails, bleached wood gives a driftwood feeling, and drives are done in crushed seashells or gravel. A "Pompeian" villa in Florida might suggest mosaic floors and Venetian glass. In all cases, clarity of concept and judgement lead to successful material choices.

In addition to materials, architecture also cues the design of details. Because the Schneiderman home was renovated in an elegant post-modern idiom, the garden required similar materials and classic, almost over-designed details. A limestone "button" motif and wainscoting, as well as columns and ironwork, were all drawn from the house and reinterpreted for the garden. In these cases, so much depends upon good team effort between the landscape architect, architect and interior designer.

Sometimes, especially in the case of rehabilitating existing landscape designs, the transition between architecture and garden is established by rigid plant forms. For instance, we retained an existing hedge of *Ilex crenata* (Japanese holly) at the Federal Reserve which is pruned almost as another piece of green marble. Such a hedge is more architecture than plant, just as a topiary is really sculpture.

The edge is where materials join forces in the garden. A well-ordered design hinges on giving thoughtful treatment to every joint and edge. Where distinct materials meet, joinery can play up the contrast. At the Vollmer Garden, for example, a sharp and angular edge at the terrace cantilevers over one end of the lily pool, accentuating the difference between the matte, blue-gray finish of stone and the dark, reflective surface of water. The pool's far edge is softly lined with smooth stones and blurred by the overlapping foliages of water-based plants.

Where materials such as terrace, lawn and border come together on the same level, the edge is often banded with a stone coping. Coping also works as a mowing strip for the wheel of a lawn mower, or as a very narrow path along a border in locations where a prominent walkway is undesirable. Coping finishes a joint; an upright edging of stone or brick holds mulch in place. Both help to keep the garden tidy.

The art of joinery applies from the tiniest detail underfoot to the way in which the entire garden meets its neighborhood and region. When a garden is oriented to a borrowed landscape, it seeks continuity with the distant view. The Rosenberg's Manhattan terrace garden is highly finished with quarry tile and painted wood because a rustic look is inappropriate to the clients' tastes and the glistening surfaces of the city view. The Gelman's suburban garden looks out on a pastoral golf course and so takes on a country feeling with stone walls and boulders.

At the Bennett/Born Garden, a confusing jumble of materials and heights were organized with lattice at a constant height. Photograph by Volkmar Wentzel.

A WORKING DESIGN

Shaping the ground itself is perhaps the most important act in building a garden. Unlike some landscape architects who sculpt the grading as a wonderful object unto itself, we try to create an unobtrusive terrain. When a landscape is flat and small, mounded planting areas contain the garden while directing the eye upward to vertical space. When a huge object like a tennis court or swimming pool has to be set into a slope, it is done for the most naturalistic effect possible. Retaining walls, whether curved or straight, are usually stone. They are semi-dry-laid, a technique which hides the mortar and permits plants to grow between the stones. Planting atop a retaining wall keeps people safely away from the edge and softens the structural mass.

Sometimes the architecture itself fails to meet the ground with grace, until built landscape elements are brought into play. A waterfall may create a dramatic setting for a house that is unmarried to its steep terrain. An "eyelid" of trellis across a blank basement wall would bring a garden up to a main floor. A looming facade might be "grounded" by a planting mound near the top of a hillside driveway.

Built elements are often dictated by legal codes that are much more concerned with safety or historic preservation than with the internal, visual needs of the garden. But codes can be "finessed" to make a design more successful. Poolside fences, for example, are usually required to be at least 42 inches tall, which can be very confining. At the Slifka Garden, a picket fence is mounted on a retaining wall of railroad ties to fool the eye into seeing a smaller fence. It also creates two different levels, separating the inner garden more effectively from the entry drive.

Limited spaces can be expanded through cleverly scaled built elements. Brick can be laid on edge in a terrace designed as a patterned carpet. This fool-the-eye trick is often done in the Netherlands, where space is at such a premium. It takes more labor and uses twice as much brick, but the results are often worth the effort and cost. Large irregular paving stones also can convey the illusion of greater space without competing, as would a more involved pattern, with plantings of lively complexity.

Built details must also account for how people will use the garden. If big parties are planned, a terrace must be adequately sized and, for safety, smoothly surfaced. On the other hand, a client who wants the soft "country" look of brick on sand needs to know that it will not be comfortable to stand on for long periods, especially in high heels. Terraces and lawns are always designed to a specific use, whether it is for children at play or 150 people dancing to a live orchestra.

Furniture is part of that picture, too. A long, low wall in a garden such as the Drapers' provides extra seating for parties. Furniture plans are sometimes worked out as part of the terrace design, not so much to suggest arrangements, but rather to determine which pieces and how many will fit comfortably in a given space. Sometimes we specify a particular style and color of furniture to suit the garden concept and materials. Freestanding benches ought to be placed in a paved alcove, whether near the front door or tucked into a far corner.

Lighting the night garden is important for all the familiar reasons. It adds festivity and drama when entertaining in the evening. It extends enjoyment of the garden past sundown for those of us who spend daylight hours during the week away from home. Lighting can transfigure the garden into an otherworldly creature that only comes out at night. But we don't install much permanent lighting, beyond providing outlets. Instead, we like to move lights around to create the moment, just like you might rearrange the lamps in your living room. Not only is the light itself ephemeral, but it is part of the fun in a changing garden to highlight a winter tree, or backlight a garden along the fence, or spotlight sculpture in the spring.

At night, lighting connects house and garden.
At the Schneiderman Garden, uplighting
the umbrella casts a reflection onto the softly lit pool.
Walls are washed with light and niches for
Phyllostachys aureosulcata (yellow-groove bamboo)
are backlit to make an elegant focal
point on axis with the dining room view, while
suggesting an enigmatic space beyond.
Photograph by Michael McKinley.

THE VITAL ELEMENT

Water is a life-giving element of all gardens, but when featured in a place of its own, it transports us to another world. Fountains are a mesmerizing source of sound and movement. They can be as simple as the splash on pavement of the German-American Friendship Garden, as deceptive as the overflowing stone drum at the Platt Garden, or as playful as a water wall where water drips from trough to trough. It is crucial to adjust the amount of flow to make the fountain sound musical.

Even the mundane swimming pool can transcend its utility when plumbed for a fountain or treated as a reflection basin with a black or white final "parging" coat. We try to make pools look as naturalistic as possible for a seamless fit into the garden. Planting up to the coping, at least on one side, strengthens its natural image, as does a shape inspired by the site. At a farm, a plump oval can look like a watering pond for cattle and horses; a long ellipse seems perfect for a "woodland pond." Steps are designed in character with the pool: tailored for a rectangle; layered along a curved edge. It is even better if the second step is designed as a bench for sitting in water up to your waist. Sometimes a top step is especially broad so that children can play at a shallow level, with parental supervision. An automatic pool cover is a wonderful luxury for securing the rectangular pool, keeping leaves and debris out, and keeping the heat in. Unfortunately, it also puts an unsightly box at one end of the pool which can sometimes be concealed with planting or a fountain wall.

Lily ponds and waterfalls give even more opportunities for naturalism in the garden. The Jacobs' pond represents a standard of construction that meets all the functional requirements, while employing certain specialized design and construction techniques for heightened realism. Made up of two pools that are on a recirculating pump, with an automatic valve that restores the optimum water level after evaporation, the pond supports a small cast of aquatic life. An acid wash safeguards fish by removing all the lime from the shot concrete and Portland cement. Three layers of waterproof black paint seal the construction.

These and other techniques go well beyond function to introduce a degree of irregularity and spontaneity that can make the most elaborate water feature seem like happenstance. A "dry stream" technique of staggered rocks is useful for fitting artificial features into the greater landscape. Most important is connecting the feature to the surrounding topography, so that water is pooling where it

Drainage is key to a garden's success. In the Schneiderman Garden, a handsome brass grate is neatly fitted to a limestone stringer at the terrace corner. Photograph by Valerie Brown.

ought to, and falling from almost random sources, with a variety of visual and sound effects.

The intensity of moving water should match the degree of slope and general mood of the place. In the Shockey garden, a system of three pools and connecting cascades changes appearance and sound as it descends a 21-foot drop. Two water sources give the Jacobs' pond the effect of a main "spring" emerging between the rocks while a secondary outlet ripples the water from another direction.

Nothing destroys a landscape design more quickly than poor drainage. Erosion horribly undercuts the paving and strands the plants. Although not a fun thing to design, "God is in the drainage," to rewrite Mies van der Rohe. Drainage is always part of a detailed garden plan. A two-percent slope on a small city terrace is as important as a whole drainage system in a hillside garden. At the International Center, a pond is designed to hold three feet of water for 45 minutes during a storm. In very contained gardens with extensive paving, such as the Schneiderman Garden, drainage is designed in a branching hierarchy starting with handsome brass grates into pipes that meet and ultimately flow into the storm sewer. The Draper Garden employs an intricate system of "French" drains—gravel-filled holes that slowly percolate water into the soil after the storm. Filter fabric lines the drain to keep soil out.

CRAFT

Sometimes even the most sophisticated gardens are still built by primitive means. In one Georgetown garden, the National Commission of Fine Arts would not permit temporary removal of a brick wall, meaning that everything had to go over by crane and the pool had to be hand-dug.

Its hairpin forms set into a concrete footing, the security fence at the International Center is made of corten steel, which develops a rusted patina. Photograph by James van Sweden.

Even obstacles such as these will not ruin the design as long as you take the time to grapple with every detail in advance. Working models and field work are pivotal factors. A terrace might be laid out in a craftsman's garage before bringing the materials to the garden. The location for a lily pond is staked in the field, rather than merely sited on a plan. The actual waterfall is "mocked up" by layering the stones and pouring water to see how it flows over the avenues provided by the design.

Simplicity is always important. In a rustic setting, the question may be how to get down a hill in the simplest way. Where budget is no object, it takes time to figure out how to make a garden lavish enough, but with taste and restraint. When in doubt, always use the simplest forms and materials available.

Some of the best built elements are those that serve many purposes, like the fence at the International Center. At once contextual and functional, its hairpin form refers to Victorian prototypes while its structure is a high-level security device for a sensitive compound of diplomatic missions. Computer tests show that it will stop a seven-ton truck at 70 miles per hour; it is even difficult to climb because it doesn't have any cross members to give a foothold. The fence traverses a hillside and manages a curve or a corner gracefully, but otherwise doesn't call much attention to itself. Made of corten steel that rusts handsomely, its stain even gives the concrete footing a touch of the ephemeral. This fence exemplifies the many contributions of a serviceable detail.

A Gallery of Built Elements

 CONCRETE

 BLUESTONE

 BRICK

 NATURAL STONE

 WOOD MEMBER

 WOOD MEMBER END

 GRAVEL

 SAND

 STONEDUST

 REINFORCING BAR

 WELDED-WIRE MESH

 FILTER FABRIC

 EXPANSION JOINT

 COMPACTED SOIL

 PLANTING SOIL

GATES, FENCES, WALLS

The sun always shines in Evelyn Nef's office garden thanks to a bit of painted shadowplay suggested by the architect Hugh Jacobsen. A diagonal line extends the darker shade of gray from the north panel (right) to cast a simulated shadow. Photograph by Oehme, van Sweden and Associates.

A wooden gate and storage structure were designed by architect Tom Stohlman to match the Drapers' Federal period home. Materials include a slate roof and redwood siding and gates painted in a traditional shade of black-green. Photograph by Volkmar Wentzel.

A window in the redwood gate to the Bennett/Born Garden. Photograph by Oehme, van Sweden and Associates.

Redwood fence and stucco wall in the Platt Garden. Photograph by Michael McKinley.

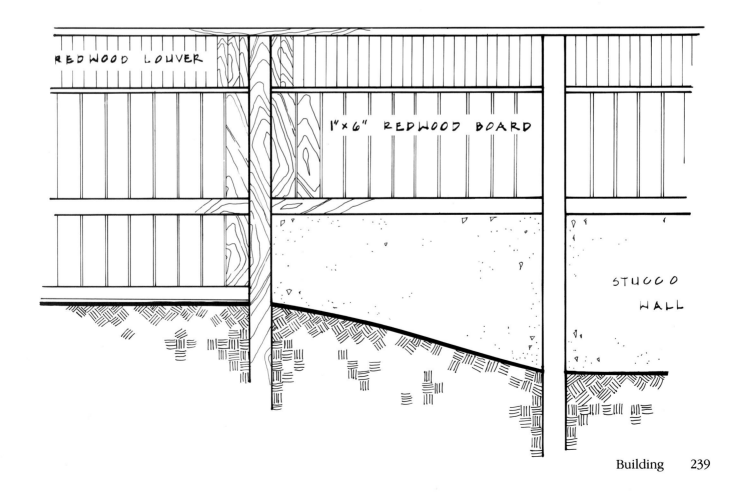

REDWOOD LOUVER

1" x 6" REDWOOD BOARD

STUCCO HALL

Wooden fence and gate in the Slifka
Garden. Photograph by James van
Sweden.

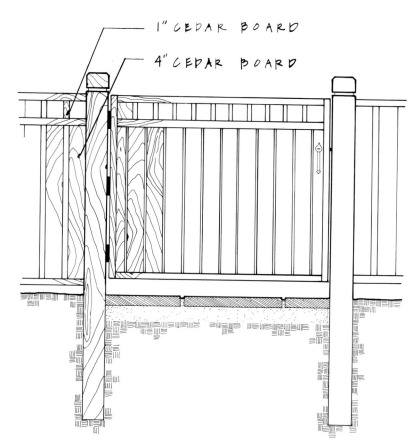

1" CEDAR BOARD

4" CEDAR BOARD

PAVING, EDGING

PLANTING BED

GRANITE PAVER

CONCRETE TROUGH

GRAVEL DRIVE

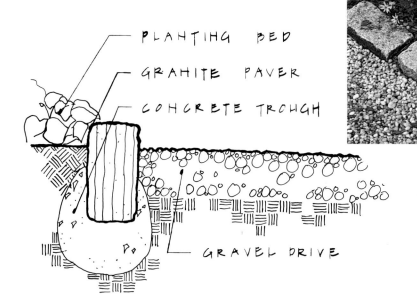

Granite cobbles edge the driveway in
the Slifka Garden. Photograph by
James van Sweden.

Dash-dot-dash brick dividers give an interesting rhythm to the bluestone path in Evelyn Nef's office garden. Two-foot squares are laid in bluestone dust. Photograph by Volkmar Wentzel.

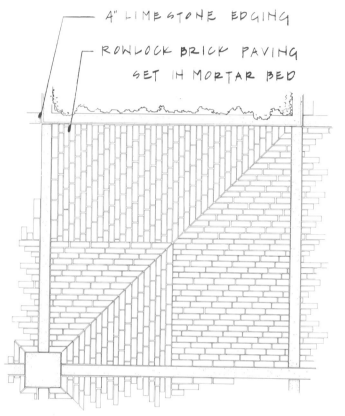

4" LIMESTONE EDGING

ROWLOCK BRICK PAVING
SET IN MORTAR BED

Brick and limestone terrace in the Schneiderman Garden. Photograph by Michael McKinley.

Setting bluestone flagging in pea gravel allows for a charming invasion of various creeping plants, including *Thymus praecox, Mazus reptans,* and *Sedum,* with an occasional *Impatiens* hybrid, in the Anne Lloyd Garden. Photograph by Paul C. De Georges.

Granite paving in the German-American Friendship Garden. Photograph by James van Sweden.

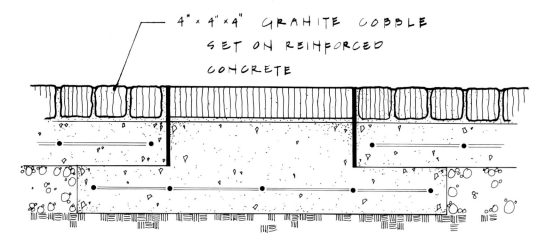

4" × 4" × 4" GRANITE COBBLE SET ON REINFORCED CONCRETE

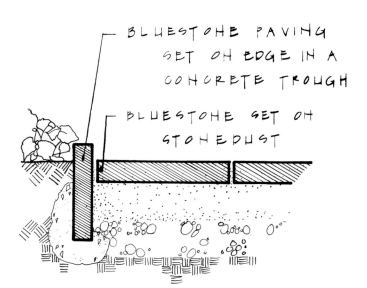

BLUESTONE PAVING
SET ON EDGE IN A
CONCRETE TROUGH

BLUESTONE SET ON
STONEDUST

Bluestone border and edging in the Gelman Garden. Photograph by Michael McKinley.

Simple squares of bluestone are randomly set into a landing of lawn between two paved terraces at the Washington, D.C., Littlefield Garden. Laid on a 4-inch-deep bed of bluestone dust, the 2 × 2-foot pavers help connect the two flights of bluestone steps visually. The carpet of lawn is designed for the family's bull mastiff dog, Nellie, who loves to roll on the soft turf. Photograph by James van Sweden.

STEPS

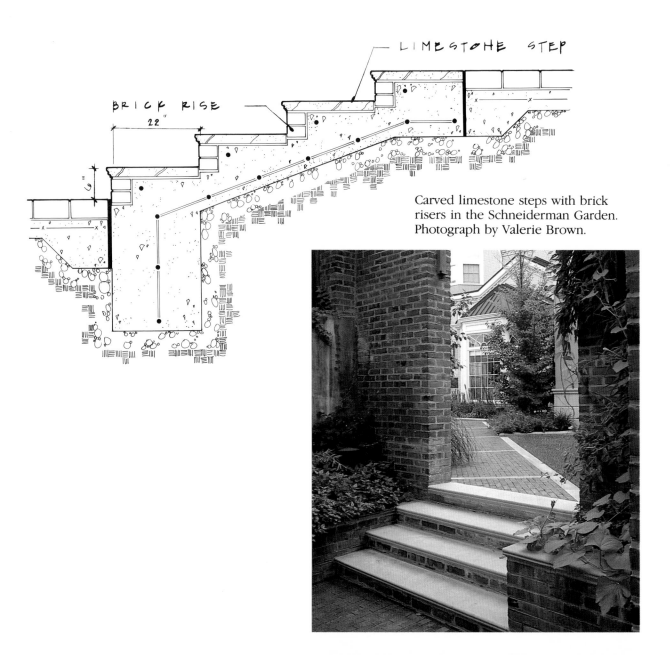

BRICK RISE
22"
LIMESTONE STEP
6"

Carved limestone steps with brick risers in the Schneiderman Garden. Photograph by Valerie Brown.

PLANTING SOIL

GRAVEL FILL FOR DRAINAGE

Semi-dry-laid wall of Stoneyhurst flagging, a local stone, in the Gelman Garden. Photograph by James van Sweden.

Brick-faced wall and matching risers with bluestone cap in a Georgetown garden. Photograph by Michael Mc-Kinley.

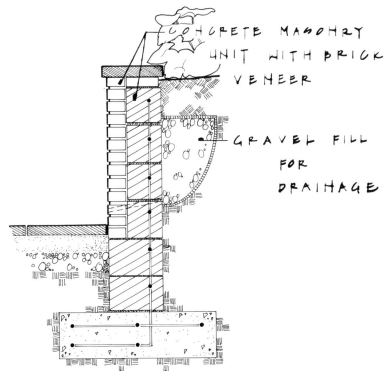

CONCRETE MASONRY UNIT WITH BRICK VENEER

GRAVEL FILL FOR DRAINAGE

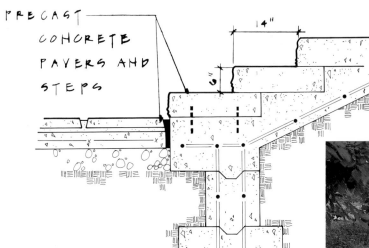

PRECAST CONCRETE PAVERS AND STEPS

14"

6"

Concrete steps in the Shockey Garden were cast from a mold of a limestone step carved with a rough-hewn riser. Beige tinting matches the lighter shade of terrace pavers. Photograph by Michael McKinley.

WATER FEATURES

Bluestone and brick fountain in the
Woodward Garden. Photograph by
John Neubauer.

COPPER
TUBING

RECIRCULATING PUMP

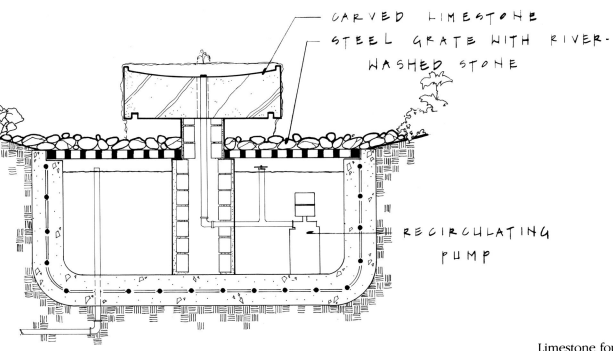

CARVED LIMESTONE

STEEL GRATE WITH RIVER-WASHED STONE

RECIRCULATING PUMP

Limestone fountain in the Platt Garden. Photograph by Volkmar Wentzel.

Axial does not necessarily mean formal. This generously elliptical lily pool is on center with the Evans house, yet the formality is softened by relaxed planting design. Photograph by John Neubauer.

Designed for children's safety, an underwater grid of PVC pipe is supported by brackets at the edge of the pool and can be easily lifted for cleaning. Aquatic plants grow up through the grid and fish enjoy swimming through it; the grid also protects fish from cats and racoons. Photograph by James van Sweden.

Lily pool in the Jacobs Garden.
Photograph by Saxon Holt.

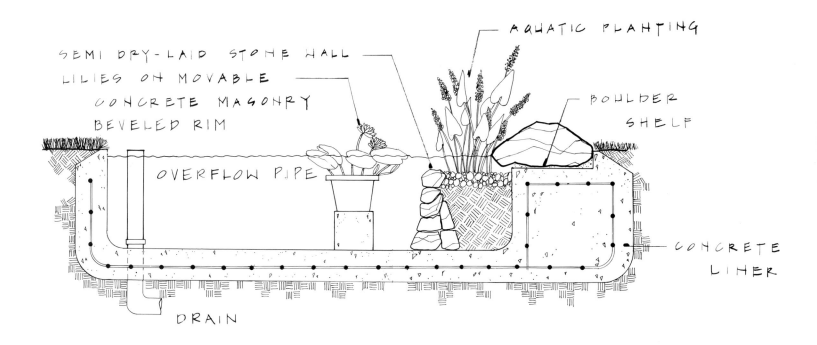

AQUATIC PLANTING

SEMI DRY-LAID STONE WALL
LILIES ON MOVABLE
CONCRETE MASONRY
BEVELED RIM

BOULDER
SHELF

OVERFLOW PIPE

CONCRETE
LINER

DRAIN

FURNISHINGS

An edging of brick simply widens into a panel to create a niche for a pristinely white Chippendale-style bench in the Smith Garden. Photograph by Michael McKinley.

Designed with the sculptor Martin Puryear, this bench is fabricated in metal to curve around a terrace at Chevy Chase Garden Plaza, Bethesda, Maryland. Photograph by Michael McKinley.

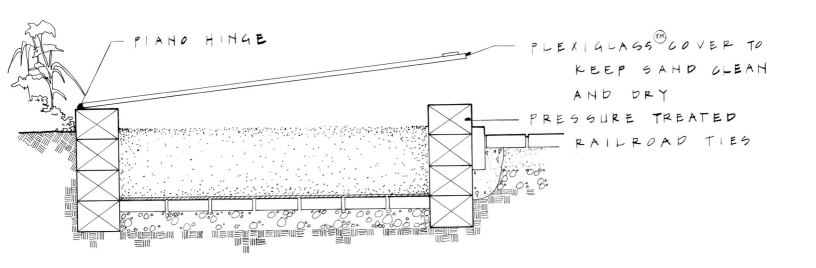

PIANO HINGE

PLEXIGLASS™ COVER TO KEEP SAND CLEAN AND DRY

PRESSURE TREATED RAILROAD TIES

Sandbox in the Smith Garden. Photograph by Michael McKinley.

A bench by the front door is an inviting element—a place to say hello or goodbye, or to sit and put on your galoshes. And because it is more comfortable to sit in a protected spot, this traditional teak bench is placed in an alcove on the brick landing at the Washington, D.C., Littlefield Garden. Photograph by James van Sweden.

Built-in bench in the Slifka Garden.
Photograph by Michael McKinley.

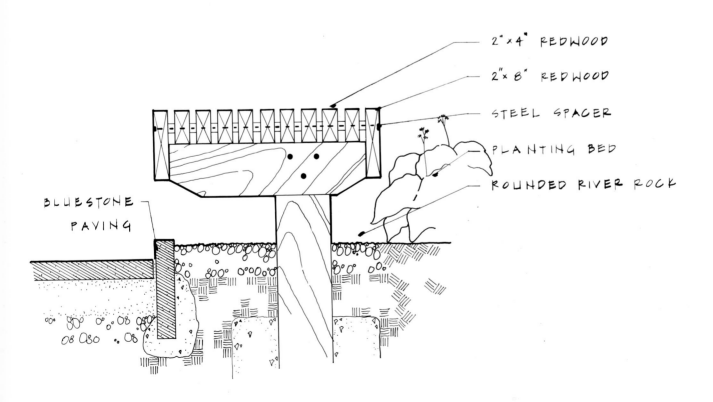

2"x 4" REDWOOD

2"x 8" REDWOOD

STEEL SPACER

PLANTING BED

ROUNDED RIVER ROCK

BLUESTONE
PAVING

TREILLAGE, ARBORS

An "eyelid" of arbor at the Slifka Garden suits the shingle-style house. Photograph by James van Sweden.

Backing a trellis with mirror reflects light and creates the illusion of a glimpse into neighboring space. Directly off the kitchen, the Smith Garden dining terrace is floored with bluestone and brick, and contains a barbecue. Photograph by Michael McKinley.

In the Jacobs Garden, finely knit lattice gives complete privacy to a bedroom suite. Slats are notched to fit together for a flush surface. Photograph by Michael McKinley.

LIGHTING

Winter lighting in the van Sweden
Garden. Photograph by John
Neubauer.

MOVABLE FIXTURE WITH
ADJUSTABLE REFLECTOR

In the Platt Garden at night, mushroom lights wash the ground plane, while spotlights catch the important plants of the season. Photograph by Michael McKinley.

Part IV

Planting

Elements of Planting Design

"T"hings are getting out of hand," a client once complained. "Grasses are growing over the path, *Rudbeckia* is seeding in the *Lavandula,* and *Lythrum* is coming up in the *Achillea!*" In Wolfgang's most militant fashion, he answered, "Move the house!" But truly, rampant growth is not a problem. It is a luxury when plants camouflage paths for several months of the year, so that you can shuffle through a "meadow." The natural look is only heightened by stray plants and blurred edges.

It is usually inadvisable to put plants in a straight line, especially when losses look like "missing teeth." Most jarring to the eye is a typical foundation planting, with round and upright plants lined up like a shooting gallery. Zigzag arrangements and larger masses are always preferable, with softer, more transparent plant selections near foundations. Evergreen hedges can be so funereal, they make the garden gloomy.

Planting design is not a formula. It is a concept based on large masses of the same plant and twelve months of interest in color and texture. Throughout the garden, intricate plantings counterpoint the broad-brush groups. Rustling grasses and bamboo create a subtle backdrop of sound, while vibrant color splashes the scene, but the major theme is variation of form and texture. The palette consists of exquisite plants which novice gardeners can easily handle, and which enthrall advanced gardeners.

Low-growing perennials are most numerous, creating a lush and undulating "ground cover." Pendulous grasses like *Pennisetum alopecuroides* may overlap and soften pools, walls and walks. Taller species (including grasses, perennials and shrubs) create a partial enclosure, while trees signal transitions and boundaries, and frame the house within the garden. Not only are you surrounded in every direction with an ever-changing panorama, but the plantings are composed so that you can see them from every side. Masses of plants undulate from low to high as

Opposite: Steps at the Taylor Garden wend through a dense, late summer border, the bluestone treads softened by various creeping *Sedum* cultivars and *Artemisia schmidtiana* 'Silver Mound'. The intense red flowers of *Hibiscus moscheutos* are brought out by a golden background of *Calamagrostis acutiflora stricta*. Vertical accents of *Yucca pendula* step back toward the finely textured *Miscanthus sinesis gracillimus* 'Haense Herms' and the massive *Miscanthus floridulus*. Photograph by Oehne, can Sweden and Associates.

Ivy trails along the stairs like a tentacle of the garden reaching toward the house. In mid-summer, each tissue-paper-like flower of *Hibiscus moscheutos* blooms nine inches in diameter. Photograph by Michael McKinley.

In mid-summer, the Vollmer Garden lily pool is a growing medium for *Iris pseudacorus* (yellow flag iris), *Sagittaria sagittifolia* var. *flore pleno* (double flowering arrowhead), *Acorus calamus* (sweet flag), *Onoclea sensibilis* (sensitive fern). *Lonicera pileata* (prostrate honeysuckle) is planted in the foreground to soften the edge. Photograph by Michael McKinley.

they move front to back and side to side, leading the eye through the composition.

Large, undifferentiated surfaces like paving, water and lawn are useful as foils to display intricate plants. Water, however, often provides another place to plant. The importance of the water plane for relief and accent determines the size and complexity of aquatic planting. Conversely, it is best to keep lawn free of trees; it is common horticultural knowledge that trees do not thrive if competing for water with the dense roots of sod. Transplanted trees grow many more roots in the first year when surrounded by mulched ground and loosely growing ground covers.

UNFOLDING IN SPACE

Layering is the key to putting you in the middle of the garden, everywhere in the garden, because the overall pattern mingles plants of all sizes. Taller plants punctuate a carpet of shorter plants throughout, as Karl Foerster advocated. For close study, more complex compositions and subtle plants are put near paved areas and contained terraces with inward views. Simpler plantings are placed in the distance, and in the foreground when outward views are most significant. Annuals are planted in pots for heady doses of color.

Planting design begins with the structural elements of trees and shrubs. These establish the garden's framework of canopy and edges, screen views, subdivide the space, provide focal points, and set forth lines to flow throughout the garden. Wherever possible, it is best to retain mature trees and rejuvenate them with careful pruning. We can learn so much from the Japanese in regard to enhancing a tree by clarifying its structure. Often, old trees must be "limbed up" to reopen views; their placement is a great help in locating border edges. Deciduous trees of open, refined forms are used to soften architecture. Shrubs are often evergreen, placed to screen the street and neighboring aspects. Seasonal considerations for selecting trees and shrubs include summer shade, the winter structure of evergreens and bare trees, and highlights of color and texture in bloom, berry, leaf and bark.

The second stage of design fills in the ground plane with predominantly herbaceous perennials. Comprising sixty to eighty percent of the total plant material in our gardens, these are the dynamic plants in nature. They return from the dead each year to amaze us with their prodigious growth. A landscape without herbaceous plants is unnatural, because it is isolated from the energy and rhythm of the seasons.

We broadly define the entire lower level of plants as a "ground cover," ranging from three inches to eight feet tall. Within the ground cover, the lower, broad masses are interconnected by overweaving groups of taller, sculptural specimens. These exclamation points create tension, balance and rhythm, subdividing the planting into internal layers that change with the seasons. While the overall scale may change, the relative proportions of plant masses do not. Our final step in achieving a dynamic, sculptural effect is never to rely on the paper plan, but to personally place plants on site.

A hillside of the International Center Southeast Quadrant takes on the quality of a color-field painting, planted with naturalistic sweeps of *Narcissus* beneath *Liriodendron tulipifera* (tulip tree) and *Quercus* species (oak). Photograph by Volkmar Wentzel.

Hillside plantings are designed to gain an illusion of depth and movement. On steep slopes, we layer plant masses according to color and texture, like a woven textile. It is almost possible to see the plants in plan, even as people drive by, because the composition is tilted upward, resembling a color field painting by Helen Frankenthaler.

EVOLVING IN TIME

No garden scene remains the same over time. Just as the garden is a moving picture that scrolls through space, so too does it advance through the seasons. The scale is constantly changing as every layer, every plant follows its own time-table of growth and decline. Although deciduous trees and shrubs shed leaves, their structure is constant; whereas the "ground cover" and "punctuation marks" fulfill a never-ending choreography of appearance and disappearance.

Bringing the ephemeral, painterly quality of planting design to the fore requires thinking in terms of succession and simultaneity. In successional planning, different plants share one space but give their display at different points in time. For instance, the spring-blooming *Dicentra specta-bilis* (bleeding-heart) could be followed with *Hosta* culti-vars (plantain lily) which send up flowers in late summer, succeeded in autumn by *Anemone japonica* (Japanese anemone). A more complicated mixture occurs when the purple wands of *Liatris spicata* emerge mysteriously from the lemon-yellow flowering *Coreopsis verticillata* 'Moon-beam', which later hosts the violet-blue haze of *Perovskia atriplicifolia*.

Simultaneous effects are a contrasting mix of color, form and texture among plants that share the same time and space. One pleasing combination occurs when the sharp, fibrous *Yucca filamentosa* studs a field of the

The essential planting design—
Sedum x *telephium* 'Autumn Joy' as a
ground-cover, pierced with sculptural textures
of *Yucca filamentosa* in the foreground
and *Molinia arundinaceae* 'Windspiel' at center
right, against a band of *Miscanthus sinensis
purpurascens*—all in a balance of evergreen and
herbaceous plants. The Rosenberg Garden, autumn.
Photograph by Ken Druse.

fleshy, round-leaved *Sedum* x *telephium* 'Autumn Joy.'
Another favorite association combines *Mazus reptans*
with *Iris sibirica* (Siberian iris).

CARE

There is no such thing as a "maintenance free" garden.
Every garden requires care and tending, or it ceases to be
a garden. Maintenance is a constant struggle, so the more
undemanding the plants, the better. Careful plant selection
makes it possible to reduce the maintenance to a level
that a homeowner can manage in spare moments, without
hiring someone to mow, weed, trim and prune every week.
The basic strategy is to choose the right plants, give them
a proper start, and let them take over.

We use elite plants, carefully selected by horticulturists
to be self-reliant and aesthetically remarkable in several
ways, such as foliage, color, flower and form. Many are
drought-tolerant. In low-maintenance design, we group
plants according to similar requirements for water and soil
type. Preparing the soil of the entire garden, lawn and all,
makes a visible difference in the overall lushness of growth.
Heavy mulch reduces weeds and watering in warm weather
(gravel mulch is cleaner at poolside). Good drainage is
especially important in winter. During the first few years,
automated irrigation (every other night) and a feeding
program of fish emulsion and time-release fertilizer gives
the garden every advantage in becoming quickly and well
established.

All these plants grow freely—but according to plan.
Ornamental grasses develop in clumps. They may need
division about once in a decade but always attain a predictable height without the "help" of pruning sheers. Competition among the plants is rarely a problem. They will fight
it out and usually call it even, because they mature at about
the same rate. Plus, once established, they are so dense that
they crowd out most weeds. Major maintenance is a twice-
yearly job. In early spring just before the spurt of growth,
dried grasses are cut down, mulch is spread, and plants are
fertilized. In addition to normal autumn clean-up, mulch
is top-dressed and bulbs are planted. Otherwise, just let
the garden go and be what it wants to be. There is no need
for staking, pruning, deadheading or mowing. All the plants
ask of us is a new appreciation for aging, as seedheads set
and dried stalks burnish through the winter months.

Low maintenance must be a viable concept for gardens
if this nation is ever to achieve a humane public landscape.
Public projects call for an especially tough and disease

resistant planting list, together with planned maintenance. It is an important part of a landscape architect's services to provide written maintenance schedules for all public projects—plant by plant and month by month—so that the maintenance staff or contractor can see exactly what to do in every plant season. They will not cut down the beautiful winter garden in late autumn; they will feed each plant properly and allow it to develop in its natural form. It is such a profound change in attitude to stop hacking plants into shaped balls and boxes that it normally takes a full year before people can accept that the garden is its own creature. Two other dividends impress maintenance professionals. First, ornamental grasses repel dogs and especially rats, whose burrows are invaded by the tough roots. Second, people are less inclined to steal plants that look so natural in their settings.

In the case of private gardens, the primary maintenance consideration is whether or not the client is a gardener. When clients claim to like gardening, it is often a fantasy. How much study and hard work will they really do? Weeding and watering are important and satisfying interactions with the garden, but these activities do not a gardener make. The gardener is creatively involved and knows what to do or not to do with the garden at all times. It is an active relationship. Planting plans for non-gardeners are generally simpler and use fewer varieties. Most of our clients employ a garden service on a weekly or seasonal basis, and rely on an in-ground, automatic irrigation system.

A gardener's garden, on the other hand, must allow flexible room for additions and experimentation. The designer is more yielding, too—more willing to give in to a whim for a particular kind of plant. We know a gardener will take the interest and the time to keep it going Such clients view the garden as an ongoing collaboration, periodically consulting with the designer.

Just as in public gardens, private garden owners must understand and respect the design's integrity. When a garden is first installed, it looks unfinished. But "what you see is not what you get," as we often say. Virtually all plants require a maturation period before the garden is complete. Some plants, like bulbs, are not even visible until the following spring. Helping clients to understand that change is the garden's dominant feature calls for constant education and reassurances.

Architecture is like a beautiful car—perfect until it rolls out of a showroom and begins to depreciate. But planting is just a newborn baby. It grows and gets better every year. Plants really are like children: think of them that way and you will know when to intervene and when

When planted in large containers, annuals
contribute bright color and continual
bloom without disturbing the perennials. A pot
at the Offutt Garden is designed as a bouquet, with
the trailing stems of a *Vinca major* 'Variegata'
(variegated annual vinca) and *Lantana montevidensis*
(weeping lantana), counterbalancing the
upright form of *Lantana camara*(pink sage).
A third shade of pink is provided by
Petunia x *hybrida* (hybrid garden petunia).
Photograph by Michael McKinley.

to leave them alone. You can develop a second sense for
what a plant wants by observing it from day to day. As plants
grow and respond to human intervention, people often get
excited and interested. It is important not to take the garden
so seriously that you kill it with kindness, but instead to
relax and have fun. With such an attitude, a person's life
may be changed by the garden.

A GROWING PALETTE

Before beginning the planting design, we ask every client
to list their favorite plants. Then we can decide if the plants
will work, given the climate and the client's ability to care
for their special needs. Invariably, if we are designing during the three spring days when weeping cherries are in
bloom, the client must have one. That is okay, because it is
a fine tree. Client's preferences give each garden a special
quality and help us to stretch the planting palette.

We are constantly seeking to introduce new plants into
our designs. Certain plants will always be associated with
the places where we found them, such as the "Dusseldorf
plant"—*Senecio doria* (groundsel)—which we first saw at
a German exhibition in 1985. After four years, we were
finally able to get it here.[10] It is a new form of goldenrod
in a bright orange yellow, which nicely complements *Rudbeckia fulgida* 'Goldsturm'. Of course, plants that are developed in other climates have to be tested here for several
years to see how they grow and what they need to flourish.

In considering a new plant, we look for "natural" habit
and distinctive texture. The plant should be rugged and
tough, resistant to drought and heat. Although we are not
too concerned about color, the plant should bloom for at
least six to eight weeks.

Fortunately, the nursery trade is enthusiastic and re-
ceptive to new and different plants. In the 'Fifties, people
wanted evergreens. They did not think in seasonal terms.
The shift toward naturalistic gardens in recent years began
with the ecology and liberation movements of the 'Sixties.
Now students, designers and gardeners are getting excited
about knowing herbaceous and deciduous plants again.
Nature is returning to the garden.

Overleaf: Drama and scale define the
"New World" garden—a
windblown collage of blurred edges and
"stained-glass" backlighting—achieved when
perennials are planted in flowing masses
and sculptural specimens punctuate the space.
Photograph by James van Sweden.

The golden days of matured grasses light up
the Shockey Garden in late fall. *Viburnum sieboldii*
(Siebold viburnum) gives the balance of
woody structure to a hillside planting of *Sedum* x
telephium 'Autumn Joy', backed by *Pennisetum
alopecuroides,* with *Miscanthus sinensis gracillimus* on
the left. Photograph by Michael McKinley.

USDA Plant Hardiness Zone Map

Agricultural Research Service, USDA, 1990

Glossary of Favorite Plants

Knowing plants is the key to making a garden that sustains itself over the years. This glossary lists just a few of the plants we favor for their toughness, versatility and seasonal effects. Because there are several authorities on plant names and horticultural requirements, not necessarily in agreement, the glossary relies ultimately on our own practical experience in different climate zones and situations.

Each description consists of text and photograph, cross-referenced to a page showing the plant in another season or within an overall planting design. The plants are divided into three categories—(1)Perennials; (2) Grasses & Sedges; and (3) Trees, Shrubs and Vines. Within each category, plants are listed alphabetically by botanical names, made up of genus, species and, if appropriate, variety. The botanical name is a plant's only accurate means of identification. Common names, which are colorful but vary widely, appear in parentheses.

On the second line, the "Type"—herbaceous, deciduous or evergreen—tells whether or not the plant's foliage persists through winter (varying according to climate). The "Family" name relates each plant to its larger category, or "genera," based on similar flowers or fruits. The plant's "Native Range" is its geographical homeland, and yields a clue as to the climatic zones in which it grows successfully, defined by the United States Department of Agriculture (U.S.D.A. Zones). Average height is given in relation to the proper spacing between plants to avoid overplanting. The text goes on to describe "Conditions," "Characteristics," and "Use." Light requirements include "partial shade," meaning morning sun and afternoon shade, and "partial sun," meaning morning shade and afternoon sun.

Where mentioned, the acidity or alkalinity of soil is vital to the plant's ability to thrive. Soils are easily tested and modified for pH (4–6 is acid, 7 is neutral, 8–9 is alkaline). The beauty of most of these plants, however, is that they need no elaborate soil preparation beyond adding humus. Humus is organic material—decomposed vegetable matter—that adds the life of bacteria to soil, while loosening its structure to water and air circulation, providing a hospitable medium for root growth. We conduct a formal soil analysis only with reason to suspect that something is wrong. At the Federal Reserve, test borings showed that existing plants died because of hard soil and bad drainage. New plantings flourished after we twice rototilled four inches of humus to a depth of twelve inches. While we always lay down two to four inches of humus, it is not usually necessary to rototill because the structure of natural soil easily incorporates humus; three to four inches of mulch will insulate the soil and help it retain moisture.

Several terms are used to describe physical characteristics of plants. A "drupe" is a fleshy fruit containing a hard-coated seed. "Inflorescence" refers to a plant's flowering part: an "umbel" is a flat-topped inflorescence with stalks arising from the same point; a loose, long, compound flower-cluster is termed a "panicle." When a plant spreads by means of "rhizomes," it sends out horizontal roots from which grow new leaves or stems. "Running stalks" take root wherever the trailing stem touches the ground.

Bloom dates are given by season rather than month, since the book is intended for world-wide distribution, including the Southern Hemisphere. "Use" suggests various ways to deploy the plant, as a single "specimen," or

small "accent" group, along a "border" edge, in large "masses," or as a "groundcover." Since planting design is a composition, the "in association with" section lists some of the most compatible perennials.

Spring bulbs play a crucial role in bridging from late-winter to the new growing season. Their foliage and flowers mask the cut-down stubble of ornamental grasses and spray the garden with color. Although we do use *Narcissus,* the biggest show is given by the *Tulipa,* which we treat like annuals to ensure the most exuberant display. We favor the red, orange and yellow 'Emperor' and, for later and longer-lasting bloom, the lily-flowering 'Red Shine', 'Jacqueline', and 'West Point'. Other choice bulbs include the elegant *Allium giganteum* (ornamental onion) and *A. aflatunense* (flowering onion), the blue-spiked *Camassia cussiki* (quamash) and the romantic *Fritillaria persica* (Persian fritillary). We plant *Muscari armeniacum* (grape hyacinth) and *Crocus* sp. along walks for close-up viewing. Generally, a simple, bold palette is achieved by mass planting one kind of bulb, always in enough quantity so that no squirrels may eat them all. Often we simply walk around the garden with a bucket in hand, tossing bulbs upon the ground to be planted wherever they land. The desired effect is a naturalistic "splash"; our secret is digging an ample hole into which we put several bulbs for the loose look of a bouquet. Avoid planting among *Sedum* and *Calamagrostis* since they emerge early enough to cover up flowering bulbs. Bulbs associate well with *Pennisetum, Rudbeckia, Aster, Miscanthus purpurascens, Anemone,* and *Lamiastrum.* The delicate blue flowers of *Brunnera* are a sparkling groundcover for lily-flowering *Tulipa,* while *Narcissus* is especially good in combination with *Hosta* and *Ligularia.*

PERENNIALS

*Acanthus hungaricus** (bear's-breech)

Caroline Segui-Kosar

Early summer. See pages 224–225.

Family: *Acanthaceae.*
Native Range: S.E. Europe.
USDA Zones: 5–9.
Type: Herbaceous.
Height: 36 inches.
Spacing: 24 inches.

Conditions: Sun or shade, but best in partial shade as leaves tend to wilt with too much afternoon sun. Prefers well-drained soil; tolerates drought. Responds well to fertilization by producing more flowers.
Characteristics: Leaves are large, glossy green, deeply dissected and arching; drying to brown and persisting until frost, while flower spikes may remain. The *Acanthus* leaf is a classic ornamental figure in Western architecture. Mauve flowers form a showy spike in summer.
Use: Accent. Massing. Dried flower arrangements. In association with *Ceratostigma, Coreopsis, Helictotrichon.*

*Nomenclatural change noted in *Kew Bulletin,* vol. 35, p. 796, 1981. Synonyms *A. balcanicus, A. longifolius.*

Achillea filipendulina 'Parker's Variety' (fern-leaf yarrow)

Pamela Harper

Early summer. See page 199.

Family: *Compositae.*
Native Range: Asia Minor and Caucasus.
USDA Zones: 4–9.
Type: Herbaceous.
Height: 36 inches.
Spacing: 18 inches.

Conditions: Sun. Prefers well-drained soil of moderate to low fertility. Drought-tolerant; does not tolerate wet soil when dormant.
Characteristics: Fine, feathery, gray-green foliage with long-lasting, flat-topped, mustard-yellow flower clusters in early summer; winter persistent.
Use: Border. Massing. Good for cut flowers and dried arrangements. In association with *Helenium, Nepeta, Pennisetum, Rudbeckia, Salvia, Veronica.*

*Aralia racemosa**
(American spikenard)

Mid-summer. See page 172.

Mid-autumn.

Family: *Araliaceae.*
Native Range: Eastern North America.
USDA Zones: 4–9.
Type: Herbaceous.
Height: 4–5 feet.
Spacing: 4 feet.

Conditions: Sun to partial shade. Prefers fertile soil with sufficient moisture.
Characteristics: Dull foliage, open form, coarse leaf borne on stalks. Greenish-white flower umbels arranged in racemes, summer blooming. Fruit and stems are colored brownish-purple to jet-black.
Use: Naturalizing. Specimen. In association with *Astilbe, Geranium, Hosta, Lamiastrum, Ligularia,* and various ferns.

*Not to be confused with the spiny, tree-form *A. spinosa.*

Artemisia schmidtiana
'Silver Mound' (silvermound wormwood)

Early summer. See page 258.

Family: *Compositae.*
Native Range: Japan.
USDA Zones: 4–8.
Type: Herbaceous.
Height: 12–18 inches.
Spacing: 18 inches.

Conditions: Sun. Will die out unless excellent drainage is provided. Trim foliage every few weeks to encourage new growth.
Characteristics: Finely-cut silvery foliage with rounded, mound-like form. Valued primarily for color and texture of foliage.
Use: Borders. Edging. Massing. Rock gardens. Slopes. In association with *Nepeta, Sedum.*

Aster x *frikartii** 'Moench'
(Michaelmas daisy)

Mid-summer. See page 146.

Family: *Compositae.*
Native Range: Europe, Asia.
USDA Zones: 5–8.
Type: Herbaceous.
Height: 30 inches.
Spacing: 18 inches.

Conditions: Sun to partial shade. Well-drained soil, especially when dormant.
Characteristics: Bright green foliage. Long-lasting, clear lavender-blue flowers from mid-summer through mid-autumn. Color blends well with yellows and whites.
Use: Border. Massing. In association with *Achillea, Artemisia, Chrysanthemum, Pennisetum, Spodiopogon.*

*Hybrid of *A. amellus* x *A. thomsonii.*

Astilbe taquetii 'Purpurkerze' (false spiraea)

Volkmar Wentzel

Mid-summer. See page 202.

Family: *Saxifragaceae.*
Native Range: E. China.
USDA Zones: 4–9.
Type: Herbaceous.
Height: 36 inches.
Spacing: 18–24 inches.

Conditions: Sun to partial shade. Moist, well-drained soil. More drought-tolerant than *A.* x *arendsii.*
Characteristics: Interesting, glossy olive-green, fine-textured leaves. Beautiful, feathery reddish-purple flower spikes—very upright for this species—appear in late summer.
Use: Dried flower plumes make it an excellent choice for autumn and winter landscapes. Massing. Borders. In association with *Begonia, Hosta, Ligularia,* and ferns.

*Begonia grandis** (hardy begonia)

Michael McKinley

Mid-autumn. See page 99.

Family: *Begoniaceae.*
Native Range: Malay, China, Japan.
USDA Zones: 6–9.
Type: Herbaceous.
Height: 12–18 inches.
Spacing: 18 inches on center.

Conditions: Partial shade. Moist, well-drained soil. Sheltered location—mulch in winter in colder zones.
Characteristics: Leaves are coppery-green above and deep red on the underside. Pale pink or white flowers held loosely above the leaves in early to mid-autumn. Spreads prolifically by bulblets and seed.
Use: Massing. Specimen. In association with *Astilbe, Hosta, Ligularia,* and various ferns.

*Synonyms B. discolor; B. evansiana.

*Bergenia cordifolia** (heartleaf bergenia)

Valerie Brown

Mid-spring. See page 130.

Pamela Harper

Mid-autumn.

Family: *Saxifragaceae.*
Native Range: Siberia and Mongolia.
USDA Zones: 3–8.
Type: Evergreen.
Height: 18 inches.
Spacing: 18–24 inches.

Conditions: Sun to partial shade. Well-drained soil.
Characteristics: Coarsely-textured, shiny, cabbage-like leaves, turning yellow, scarlet and purple in autumn, persisting into winter. Magenta-pink flowers in early spring.
Use: Contrast with *Yucca* and other sword-like foliage. Groundcover. Massing. In association with *Astilbe, Epimedium, Liriope.*

*Formerly Saxifraga cordifolia.

Brunnera macrophylla*
(perennial forget-me-not)

Pamela Harper

Mid-spring. See page 110.

Family: *Boraginaceae.*
Native Range: W. Caucasus and Siberia.
USDA Zones: 4–8.
Type: Herbaceous.
Height: 12–18 inches.
Spacing: 18 inches.

Conditions: Shade to partial shade. Prefers moist soil, although tolerates dry shade.
Characteristics: Large, heart-shaped leaves. Spring-blooming, vivid blue sprays of forget-me-not-like flowers. Self-seeding.
Use: Groundcover. Naturalizing in woodland areas. In association with *Astilbe, Ligularia, Liriope,* and various ferns.

*Formerly *Anchusa myosotidiflora.*

Caryopteris x clandonensis*
(hybrid bluebeard)

Caroline Segui-Kosar

Late summer. See page 139.

Family: *Verbenaceae.*
Native Range: Japan to N.W. China.
USDA Zones: 5–9.
Type: Woody sub-shrub.
Height: 24–30 inches.
Spacing: 30–36 inches.

Conditions: Sun to partial sun. Loose, well-drained soil. Drought-tolerant. Cut back in late winter six inches from the ground to promote flowering on new growth.
Characteristics: Gray-green foliage. Brilliant, silvery-blue flowers in late summer.
Use: Massing. Contrasting color with late-season perennials. In association with *Calamagrostis, Panicum, Pennisetum, Perovskia, Sedum, Spodiopogon, Stachys.*

*Hybrid developed by Arthur Simmonds at West Clandon, Surrey, England, from *C. incana* x *C. mongholica.*

Ceratostigma plumbaginoides*
(blue leadwort)

Michael McKinley

Late summer. See page 138.

Family: *Plumbaginaceae.*
Native Range: W. China.
USDA Zones: 5–8.
Type: Herbaceous.
Height: 12 inches.
Spacing: 12–18 inches.

Conditions: Sun to partial shade. Fertile, well-drained soil. Tolerates drought. Provide light winter mulch in colder zones.
Characteristics: Red foliage and brilliant blue flowers in autumn. Once established, spreads freely by underground rhizomes. May be late to re-emerge in spring.
Use: An excellent groundcover for hot locations. Front border. In association with *Coreopsis, Liriope, Panicum, Pennisetum, Sedum, Yucca.*

*Synonym *Plumbago larpentiae.*

Coreopsis verticillata 'Moonbeam' (threadleaf coreopsis)

Mid-summer. See page 92.

Family: *Compositae.*
Native Range: E. United States.
USDA Zones: 3–9.
Type: Herbaceous.
Height: 18–24 inches.
Spacing: 18 inches.

Conditions: Sun to partial shade. Prefers well-drained soil, although tolerates most conditions.
Characteristics: Airy, fern-like foliage in compact clumps. Small, lemon-yellow flowers bloom from early to late summer.
Use: Border. Massing. In association with *Helictotrichon, Liatris, Perovskia.*

Epimedium x versicolor* 'Sulphureum' (Persian epimedium)

Late spring. See page 243.

Family: *Berberidaceae.*
Native Range: Asia.
USDA Zones: 5–9.
Type: Herbaceous.
Height: 12 inches.
Spacing: 12–18 inches.

Conditions: Partial shade or sun (if given ample moisture). Prefers cool shady location and well-drained soil.
Characteristics: Foliage takes on a reddish-bronze cast in late summer, winter-persistent through zone 7. Loose sprays of sulphur-yellow flowers in early spring.
Use: Mass planting. Groundcover under trees and shrubs. In association with *Anemone, Astilbe, Bergenia, Liriope.*

*Hybrid of *E. grandiflorum* x *E. pinnatum.*

Eupatorium purpureum* 'Gateway' (Joe-Pye weed)

Mid-summer. See pages 204–205.

Family: *Compositae.*
Native Range: North America.
USDA Zones: 5–9.
Type: Herbaceous.
Height: 5–6 feet.
Spacing: 3–4 feet.

Conditions: Full sun to partial shade. Prefers moist soil; once established, resists drought.
Characteristics: Showy flowers of fuzzy, purplish clusters on purple stems. Attracts butterflies.
Use: Back border. Wetland. Meadow. Naturalizing. In association with *Calamagrostis, Lythrum, Miscanthus, Senecio.*

*Synonym *E. fistulosum*

Hemerocallis liliaceae
'Stella d'Oro' (daylily)

Oehme, van Sweden

Early summer. See page 194.

Family: *Liliaceae.*
Native Range: Central Europe to Japan.
USDA Zones: 4–9.
Type: Semi-evergreen.
Height: 2–3½ feet.
Spacing: 18–24 inches.

Conditions: Sun to partial shade. Prefers moist, well-drained soil, although quite tolerant. Resists heat and drought.
Characteristics: Narrow, dark green foliage. Bright yellow, lightly scented flowers held high. 'Stella d'Oro' is one of the longest blooming of the repeat-blooming *Hemerocallis* species.
Use: Border. Massing. Naturalizing. In association with *Achillea, Calamagrostis, Lythrum, Pennisetum, Rudbeckia.*

Hibiscus moscheutos
(common rose mallow)

John Neubauer

Late summer. See page 258.

Family: *Malvaceae.*
Native Range: United States.
USDA Zones: 5–10.
Type: Herbaceous.
Height: 3–6 feet.
Spacing: 24–30 inches.

Conditions: Sun. Prefers fertile, moist soil, although *H.moscheutos* is more tolerant of dry, sandy conditions than most other species. A winter mulch in cooler zones may be necessary.
Characteristics: Strikingly big, soft green foliage. Huge, satiny flowers up to six inches in diameter in late summer. Color range includes pink, white, red and bicolors. May be late to emerge in spring.
Use: For a tropical effect in shrub borders, perennial borders, or when naturalized near ponds or in wet meadows. In association with *Lythrum, Pennisetum, Senecio.*

*Hosta sieboldiana**
(plantain lily)

Michael McKinley

Late spring. See page 212.

Family: *Liliaceae.*
Native Range: Japan.
USDA Zones: 4–9.
Type: Herbaceous.
Height: 30 inches.
Spacing: 2 feet.

Conditions: Shade to partial shade. Prefers moist, humus-rich soil. Mulch crown with grit to avoid snail and slug damage.[11]
Characteristics: Largest leaves of any *Hosta:* 12–15 inches in diameter with blue-gray foliage and white flower stalks in spring.
Use: Massing. Near pools.

*Formerly *H. glauca.*

Hypericum calycinum*
(St.-John's-wort)

Late summer. See pages 224—225.

Family: *Hypericaceae.*
Native Range: S.E. Europe, Asia Minor.
USDA Zones: 4–9.
Type: Evergreen.
Height: 12–18 inches.
Spacing: 18–24 inches.

Conditions: Sun to partial shade.
Tolerates dry, sandy soil.
Characteristics: Dark, glossy green foliage turns purple in autumn, remaining until early spring. Bright yellow flowers in mid- to late summer. Cut back extensively in spring every few years. **Use:** Groundcover under trees. In association with *Ceratostigma, Pennisetum, Rudbeckia.*

*Formerly *H. grandiflorum.*

Liatris spicata
(gay-feather)

Early summer. See page 95.

Family: *Compositae.*
Native Range: E. United States.
USDA Zones: 5–9.
Type: Herbaceous.
Height: 24–30 inches.
Spacing: 18 inches on center.

Conditions: Sun to partial shade. Moist, well-drained soil; somewhat drought-tolerant.
Characteristics: Leafy, dark green, grass-like foliage at base. Brilliant violet spikes, 6–15 inches long, flowering from the top down.
Use: Massing. Vertical accent in lower-growing groundcover. In association with *Coreopsis, Liriope.*

Ligularia dentata* 'Desdemona'
(bigleaf goldenray)

Early summer. See pages 168–169.

Family: *Compositae.*
Native Range: China.
USDA Zones: 4–9.
Type: Herbaceous.
Height: 36–42 inches.
Spacing: 24 inches on center.

Conditions: Partial shade; leaves wilt with too much afternoon sun. Requires moist to boggy soils, where it will self-seed.
Characteristics: Large heart-shaped leaves, dark greenish-brown to silver above, maroon below. Yellow-orange, daisy-like flower. Attracts butterflies. Mulch crown with grit to avoid snail and slug damage.
Use: Massing. North and east sides of buildings. In association with *Astilbe, Hosta, Ligularia, Liriope, Lamiastrum,* and various ferns.

*Formerly *L. clivorum.*

Liriope muscari 'Big Blue' (lilyturf)

Michael McKinley

Late summer. See page 204.

Family: *Liliaceae.*
Native Range: Japan, China.
USDA Zones: 4–9.
Type: Evergreen.
Height: 12 inches.
Spacing: 12–18 inches.

Conditions: Partial sun to shade; needs more shade in hot climates. Tolerates dryness under trees after becoming established.
Characteristics: Small, clump-forming plants with dark green, grass-like foliage. Lilac-purple flowers, similar to *Muscari armeniacum* (grape hyacinth), bloom in late summer to early autumn, followed by black, bead-like fruit.
Use: Groundcover. Border. Massing under trees and shrubs. In association with *Bergenia, Caryopteris, Geranium.*

Lythrum salicaria 'Morden's Pink'* (pink loosestrife)

Pamela Harper

Early summer. See page 105.

Family: *Lythraceae.*
Native Range: North temperate regions.
USDA Zones: 4–8.
Type: Herbaceous.
Height: 3–4 feet.
Spacing: 18–24 inches.

Conditions: Sun for best flowering. Fertile soil; grows well in wet conditions.
Characteristics: Erect habit. Willow-like leaves. Bright pink flower spikes from early to late summer.
Use: Aquatic areas. Massing. Border. Accent. In association with *Hemerocallis, Hibiscus.*

*This cultivar does not produce seed, so it is not invasive like the native species recently banned to protect wetlands in some northern states.

Macleaya cordata* (plume poppy)

Michael McKinley

Mid-summer. See page 66.

Family: *Papaveraceae.*
Native Range: China, Japan.
USDA Zones: 4–9.
Type: Herbaceous.
Height: 5–9 feet.
Spacing: 3 feet.

Conditions: Sun (in cooler climates) to partial shade.
Characteristics: Large, lobed fig-like leaves. Bold, branching flower plumes of light coral to buff colors. Running stalks colonize quickly.
Use: Clump or specimen among shrubs or rear border. Excellent for naturalizing. In association with *Hemerocallis, Lythrum, Miscanthus.*

*Formerly *Bocconia cordata.*

Perovskia atriplicifolia
(Russian sage)

Mid-summer. See pages 204–205.

Family: *Labiatae.*
Native Range: Asia (Afghanistan, Tibet).
USDA Zones: 3–9.
Type: Woody sub-shrub.
Height: 3–4 feet.
Spacing: 24–30 inches.

Conditions: Sun. Well-drained soil: resists drought.
Characteristics: Aromatic. Stiffly upright, silvered woody stems rise from the base to cascade, presenting silvery-gray foliage and lavender-purple flowers from early summer to early autumn.
Use: Textural complement to lower perennials and groundcovers. In association with *Artemisia, Coreopsis, Hypericum, Liriope, Nepeta, Sedum.*

Rudbeckia fulgida 'Goldsturm'*
(black-eyed Susan)

Mid-summer. See page 57.

Late Autumn.

Family: *Compositae.*
Native Range: North America.
USDA Zones: 4–9.
Type: Herbaceous.
Height: 24 inches.
Spacing: 18–24 inches.

Conditions: Sun to partial shade. Fertile, preferably moist, soil. Will not tolerate dry conditions.
Characteristics: Sturdy, deep green, glossy-leaved plant. Long-lasting, rayed flower heads of yellow-orange with dark, black cones that persist into winter. Represents the black-eyed Susan to perfection.
Use: Masses. Small groups. In association with *Calamagrostis, Liriope, Lythrum, Pennisetum, Senecio.*

*Selected and named 'Goldsturm' by Karl Foerster in 1933 in Germany.

Salvia x *superba** 'Mainacht'
(purple sage)

Early summer. See page 158.

Family: *Labiatae.*
Native Range: Europe, Great Britain.
USDA Zones: 4–9.
Type: Herbaceous.
Height: 18–24 inches.
Spacing: 18 inches.

Conditions: Sun to partial shade. Well-drained soil.
Characteristics: Rough green foliage. Numerous spikes of strong violet-blue flowers project from a compact plant. Spent flowers should be cut back after blooming for a repeat flower production from early summer until frost.
Use: Border massing. Indigo color contrasts well with lighter-colored perennials. In association with *Coreopsis, Hemerocallis, Rudbeckia, Sedum, Senecio.*

*Formerly *S. nemerosa.*

Sedum x 'Ruby Glow'*
(stonecrop)

Mid-summer. See page 103.

Family: *Crassulaceae*.
Native Range: Japan, China, Korea.
USDA Zones: 4–9.
Type: Herbaceous.
Height: 8–12 inches.
Spacing: 12 inches.

Conditions: Sun. Dry to moderately moist soils.
Characteristics: Fleshy gray-blue foliage turns burgundy in mid-summer. Small, pink flowers in early autumn.
Use: Groundcover. Front border. In association with *Perovskia, Salvia, Sesleria*.

*Hybrid of *Sedum cauticolum* x *S. telephium*.

Sedum x telephium
*'Autumn Joy' (live-forever)

Mid-Autumn. See page 144.

Late summer.

Family: *Crassulaceae*.
Native Range: Japan.
USDA Zones: 4–9.
Type: Herbaceous.
Height: 18–24 inches.
Spacing: 18–24 inches.

Conditions: Sun; will grow in partial shade. Very drought-tolerant.
Characteristics: The tallest *Sedum*. Interesting gray-green foliage. A four-season plant with broccoli-like buds of light green in spring, changing over the summer to light pink, to dark coppery-red, and finally to dark brown in autumn. Dried flowers persist throughout the winter and should not be cut until spring.
Use: In masses as a groundcover. Specimen in smaller groups. In association with *Ceratostigma, Coreopsis, Pennisetum, Sesleria, Yucca*.

*Hybrid of *S. spectabile* x *S. telephium*.

Yucca filamentosa
(Adam's-needle)

Early summer. See page 128.

Family: *Agavaceae*.
Native Range: S.E. United States.
USDA Zones: 4–9.
Type: Evergreen.
Height: 3–4 feet.
Spacing: 24–30 inches.

Conditions: Sun. Drought-tolerant.
Characteristics: Sword-like leaves of blue-green with thin, curling threads along the margins. Very showy, fragrant, creamy-white flower spikes on stiff, upright stems.
Use: Accent. Massing. Coarse foliage contrasts magnificently with finer-textured plants. In association with *Ceratostigma, Coreopsis, Sedum*.

*Achnatherum brachytricha**
(silver spike grass)

Wolfgang Oehme

Early autumn.

Family: *Gramineae.*
Native Range: Korea.
USDA Zones: 4–9.
Height (inflorescence): 24–30 inches.
Spacing: 18–24 inches.

Conditions: Sun to partial shade. Prefers alkaline, well-drained soil.
Characteristics: Winter-persistent. Blooms in early autumn with purple-rose inflorescence.
Use: Massing. Small clumps. Accent. In association with *Liriope, Rudbeckia, Sedum.*

*Synonym Calamagrostis brachytricha.

Calamagrostis acutiflora stricta
(feather reed grass)

Jonathan Blair

Mid-summer. See page 93.

Family: *Gramineae.*
Native Range: Europe, Britain, E. and S. Africa.
USDA Zones: 4–9.
Height: 4½–7 feet.
Spacing: 24 inches.

Conditions: Full sun to light shade (flower stalks flop over in shade). Will grow in wet or dry conditions.
Characteristics: A somewhat coarse, stout, deciduous perennial grass with narrowly erect habit. Growth starts very early in spring. Flowers show in early summer as upright panicles, drying to wheat color and persisting throughout the winter.
Use: Background. Specimen. Massing in small or large groups. In association with *Aster, Pennisetum, Rudbeckia, Sedum.*

Carex morrowii variegata
(silver variegated Japanese sedge)

Michael McKinley

Early summer.

Family: *Cyperaceae.*
Native Range: Japan.
USDA Zones: 5–9.
Height: 12 inches.
Spacing: 12 inches.

Conditions: Partial shade. Cool, moist soil.
Characteristics: Compact form. Dark, semi-evergreen foliage with narrow, silver striations. Insignificant bloom in late spring.
Use: Borders. Edging. Massing. In association with *Bergenia, Epimedium, Rodgersia pinnata.*

Carex pendula
(great drooping sedge grass)

Michael McKinley

Late spring. See page 220.

Family: *Cyperaceae.*
Native Range: Europe, N. Africa, Britain.
USDA Zones: 5–9.
Height: 24–36 inches.
Spacing: 24–30 inches.

Conditions: Full to partial shade. Prefers cool, moist, clayey soil.
Characteristics: Arching form and large, broad, pendulous leaves, yellow-green above and glaucus below. Semi-evergreen. Late spring inflorescence not showy, but with an interesting hanging, catkin-like structure.
Use: Groundcover. Vertical or textural accent among other sedge varieties. Wet, woodland areas. In association with *Astilbe, Bergenia, Epimedium, Hosta, Ligularia, Rodgersia pinnata.*

Cortaderia selloana pumila
(pampas grass)

James van Sweden

Early autumn. See page 105.

Family: *Gramineae.*
Native Range: Brasil, Argentina, Chile.
USDA Zones: 6–10.
Height: 8–12 feet.
Spacing: 4–5 feet.

Conditions: Full sun. Well-drained soil.
Characteristics: Large, dense clump of sharply-edged leaves with spectacular 12- to 24-inch, silvery, creamy-white plumes that bloom in autumn.
Use: Screening. Accent. In association with *Eupatorium, Lythrum.*

Deschampsia caespitosa
'Goldgehaenge' (tufted hair grass)

Early summer.

Family: *Gramineae.*
Native Range: N. and S. Hemispheres, Britain.
USDA Zones: 4–9.
Height: 24–36 inches.
Spacing: 30 inches.

Conditions: Sun to partial shade. Moist, acidic soil; does not tolerate dryness.
Characteristics: Densely tufted mound of dark green, slender, arching foliage. Pale-green to purple panicles turn golden-yellow in autumn.
Use: Specimen. Massing. In association with *Bergenia, Epimedium, Hosta, Ligularia.*

Fargesia murielae *
(Chinese clump bamboo)

Mid-summer. See page 66.

Family: *Gramineae.*
Native Range: China.
USDA Zones: 4–9.
Height: 10–12 feet.

Conditions: Shade to partial shade; requires more shade in hot climates. Ample moisture. Sheltered location.
Characteristics: Graceful, non-invasive, evergreen to semi-evergreen. Leaves are dull, olive-green. Slow-growing. Whip-like, branchless canes in the first season, coated with a bluish-gray to rich-purple. Branches increasing and twiggy in subsequent years, until it eventually develops into a full specimen with sculptural qualities. Be patient. Should never be cut back or pruned.
Use: Specimen. Massing. Screening.

*Synonym *Sinarundinaria nitida.*

Helictotrichon sempervirens *
(blue oat grass)

Mid-summer. See page 165.

Family: *Gramineae.*
Native Range: Europe.
USDA Zones: 4–8.
Height: 24–30 inches.
Spacing: 24 inches.

Conditions: Sun to partial shade. Acidic, well-drained sandy soil.
Characteristics: Tufted, compact clump of stiff, blue-green leaves which maintain their color until early spring. Graceful, erect or nodding panicles of large spikelets.
Use: Accent. Specimen. Massing. Naturalizing. In association with *Artemisia, Nepeta, Stachys.*

*Synonym *Avena sempervirens.*

Imperata cylindrica
'Red Baron' (Japanese blood grass)

Michael McKinley

Mid-summer. See page 174.

Family: *Gramineae.*
Native Range: Japan.
USDA Zones: 5–9.
Height: 12–18 inches.
Spacing: 12–18 inches.

Conditions: Sun to partial shade. Moist, well-drained soil.
Characteristics: Brilliant scarlet foliage throughout the season, becoming more intense in autumn. Slow to become established; spreads by rhizomes.
Use: Groundcover. Accent. Specimen. In association with *Bergenia, Stachys.*

Miscanthus floridulus*
(giant Chinese silver grass)

Peter Jones

Mid-Autumn. See page 258.

Family: *Gramineae.*
Native Range: Asia.
USDA Zones: 4–9.
Height: 10–12 feet.
Spacing: 5–8 feet.

Conditions: Full sun. Sufficient moisture; will be stunted in dry locations and lower leaves will brown.
Characteristics: A vigorous, clump-forming giant grass. Very upright in character with long leaf blades. Blooms in late fall (may not bloom in colder regions). Allow to stand in winter until wind blows away leaves and only stalks remain.
Use: Bold, architectural specimen in lawn. Screening. Rear of large border. In association with *Hibiscus, Rudbeckia.*

*Formerly *M. sinensis giganteus.*

Miscanthus sinensis gracillimus*
(maiden grass)

James van Sweden

Mid-Autumn. See page 129.

Family: *Gramineae.*
Native Range: China, Japan.
USDA Zones: 4–9.
Height: 4–6 feet.
Spacing: 3–4 feet on center.

Conditions: Sun. Needs sufficient moisture for flowers to develop; once established, tolerates dryness.
Characteristics: Elegant, arching habit of growth. This variety has a finely textured leaf with conspicuous mid-vein of white. Flowers bloom in late autumn, held high above foliage.
Use: Backdrop. Screening. Vertical accent with low groundcovers. In association with *Aster, Pennisetum, Rudbeckia, Sedum.*

*New varieties from Ernst Pagels in Leer, Ostfriesland, Germany, include 'Malepartus', 'Graziella', 'Roland', 'Zwergelefant', 'Wetterfahne', 'Grosse Fontaene', 'Goliath', 'Positano'.

Miscanthus sinensis purpurascens
(purple silver grass)

Volkmar Wentzel

Mid-Autumn. See page 170.

Family: *Gramineae.*
Native Range: Himalayas.
USDA Zones: 4–9.
Height: 4–5 feet.
Spacing: 36 inches.

Conditions: Full sun. Moist, well-drained soil; not drought tolerant.
Characteristics: Handsome, compact form of *Miscanthus.* Blooms mid-summer. Develops a combined coloration of burgundy, gold-yellow, red and purple foliage in fall, highlighting the silvery gleam of the upright flower panicles.
Use: Accent. Screening. Back of border. In association with *Rudbeckia, Sedum, Yucca.*

Molinia arundinacea
'Transparent'* (tall purple moor grass)

Ken Druse

Early autumn. See page 263.

Family: *Gramineae.*
Native Range: Europe.
USDA Zones: 3–8.
Height: 5–6 feet.
Spacing: 36–42 inches.

Conditions: Sun. Acid soil. Sufficient moisture.
Characteristics: Long, thin, "transparent" seed stalks, shooting 3 feet or more above the mounding green foliage. Golden-yellow leaves and inflorescence in autumn.
Use: Particularly effective as a vertical accent in combination with *Coreopsis, Sedum.*

*Other notable varieties include 'Windspiel' and 'Karl Foerster'.

Panicum virgatum
'Haense Herms' (red switch grass)

Michael McKinley

Late summer. See pages 100–101.

Family: *Gramineae.*
Native Range: United States.
USDA Zones: 3–9.
Height: 36–48 inches.
Spacing: 30 inches.

Conditions: Sun. Tolerates most garden soils and drought.
Characteristics: Airy, mist-like inflorescence with a reddish tint in fall. Foliage is finely-textured; tops turn reddish in late summer, then beige in winter.
Use: Massing. Back of border. In association with *Aster, Boltonia, Sedum, Yucca.*

Pennisetum alopecuroides*
(fountain grass)

Late summer. See page 189.

Family: *Gramineae*.
Native Range: Asia.
USDA Zones: 4–9.
Height: 36 inches.
Spacing: 24 inches.

Conditions: Sun to partial shade. Moist, fertile soil; growth will be stunted if soil is too dry. May seed itself in moist conditions.
Characteristics: Handsome summer and autumn effects. Culms erect, becoming arching toward tip.
Use: Small to large groups. In association with *Aster, Eupatorium, Rudbeckia, Sedum, Yucca.*

*Another notable variety is the later-blooming 'Moudry', with dark foliage and inflorescence; *P. orientale* blooms all summer and is more delicate in shape and inflorescence.

Sesleria autumnalis
(autumn moor grass)

Late summer.

Family: *Gramineae*.
Native Range: Central Europe, Britain, Iceland.
USDA Zones: 3–8.
Height: 12–18 inches.
Spacing: 18 inches on center.

Conditions: Sun to partial shade. Alkaline, well-drained soil. Extremely drought-tolerant.
Characteristics: Small mounds of yellow-green foliage with short, silver-white to light brown panicles. Grown primarily for semi-evergreen foliage.
Use: Border massing. Woodland edges. In association with *Ceratostigma, Chrysanthemum pacificum, Sedum.*

Spodiopogon sibiricus*
(silver spike grass)

Late summer. See page 97.

Family: *Gramineae*.
Native Range: Siberia, China, Korea, Japan.
USDA Zones: 3–9.
Height: 3–4 feet.
Spacing: 30 inches.

Conditions: Sun. Tolerates drought.
Characteristics: Sculptural grass with dense, bamboo-like foliage. Flowers are distinctly separated, dark silvery-purple spikelets, blooming in mid- to late summer. Foliage turns reddish-purple to yellow in autumn; almost disappearing entirely in winter. Slow to develop when young.
Use: Specimen. Mass plantings. In association with *Aster, Rudbeckia, Sedum, Stachys.*

*Formerly *Muhlenbergia alpestris*.

TREES, SHRUBS, AND VINES

Amelanchier canadensis
(shadblow)

Mid-spring. See page 172.

Family: *Rosaceae.*
Native Range: Eastern United States.
USDA Zones: 4–9.
Type: Deciduous.
Height: 20–30 feet.

Conditions: Prefers sun, but tolerates deep shade, although producing few flowers and fruits. Moist to average, well-drained, sandy soil.
Characteristics: Multi-stemmed shrub form in the North; tree-form in the South. Gray bark. Masses of nodding, pyramidal white flowers in late spring. Maroon-purple fruits attract wildlife. Brilliant yellow in autumn with occasional highlights of red-to-orange.
Use: Woodland edge.

*Clematis paniculata**
(sweet autumn clematis)

Late summer. See pages 168–169.

Family: *Ranunculaceae.*
Native Range: Japan.
USDA Zones: 5–9.
Type: Deciduous.
Height: 30 feet.

Conditions: Partial shade. Moist, well-drained soil.
Characteristics: Lustrous, dark semi-evergreen leaves. Profuse display of bouquet-like clusters of white, fragrant flowers from late summer through early autumn. Seedheads are fluffy, silvery plumes which persist late into the season.
Use: Vine for fences, walls, arbors and treillage.

*Synonym *Clematis maximowicziana.*

Cornus kousa
(Kousa dogwood)

Early summer. See page 58.

Winter.

Family: *Cornaceae.*
Native Range: Japan, Korea, Central China.
USDA Zones: 5–8.
Type: Deciduous.
Height: 25 feet.

Conditions: Sun to partial shade. Well-drained, acidic soil. More tolerant of both drought and poor drainage than *Cornus florida.*
Characteristics: Profuse display of pure white flowers after foliage emerges in spring; blooms later than *C. florida.* Horizontal branching habit makes this a good choice for viewing from elevated positions. Exfoliating bark in mature trees adds winter interest. Stalked, red-raspberry-like fruits attract wildlife.
Use: Woodland edge.

Euonymus sachalinensis*
(Sakhalin euonymus)

Early autumn.

Family: *Celastraceae.*
Native Range: Northeastern Asia.
USDA Zones: 5–8.
Type: Deciduous.
Height: 12 feet.

Conditions: Sun to partial shade. Moist soil. Tolerates high alkalinity.
Characteristics: Small whitish-green flowers in spring. Large, red seed capsules in autumn, with pink-red fruit hanging from undersides of branches. Red to yellow fall foliage.
Use: Small groups.

*Synonym *E. planipes.*

Hamamelis x intermedia
'Arnold Promise' (witch hazel)

Mid-winter.

Late winter.

Family: *Hamamelidaceae.*
Native Range: China.
USDA Zones: 5–8.
Type: Deciduous.
Height: 15–20 feet.

Conditions: Sun to partial shade. Prefers neutral-to-acid, moist, well-drained soil.
Characteristics: Vase-shaped form, more upright than spreading. One of the earliest signs of spring color. Fragrant clusters of clear yellow flower tufts in mid-winter through early spring adorn the leafless branches. Autumn leaves are colored red-to-orange. Vigorous and faster-growing than other *Hamamelis* species.
Use: Massing. Specimen. Screening.

Hydrangea anomala
subsp. **petiolaris**
(climbing hydrangea)

Early summer.

Family: *Hydrangeaceae.**
Native Range: Himalayas, China.
USDA Zone: 4.
Type: Deciduous.
Height: 75 feet.

Conditions: Partial shade. Fertile, moist, well-drained soil.
Characteristics: A clinging, woody vine which requires some support on which to grow. Foliage is glossy green and persists late into the season. Showy flowers are white, flat-topped clusters, 6–10 inches in diameter, eventually turning a rust-color and persisting into winter. Exfoliating bark is rich cinnamon-brown to red, and provides seasonal interest.
Use: Vine for fences, walls, arbors, treillage and rockeries.

*Also included in the *Saxifragaceae* family.

Ilex x 'Nellie R. Stevens'*
(Nellie R. Stevens holly)

Mid-summer.

Family: *Aquifoliaceae.*
Native Range: Europe, W. Asia, China, Korea.
USDA Zones: 6–9.
Type: Evergreen.
Height: 15–25 feet.

Conditions: Sun to partial shade. Prefers acidic, moist, well-drained soil.
Characteristics: Pyramidal form; much denser branching and broader habit than *I. fosteri.* Glossy olive-green leaves with sharp-spined tips. Red fruit. Vigorous, relatively fast-growing.
Use: Screening.

*Hybrid of *I. aquifolium* x *I. cornuta.*

Ilex x attenuata 'Fosteri'*
(Foster holly)

Early winter. See pages 100–101.

Family: *Aquifoliaceae.*
Native Range: North America.
USDA Zones: 6–9.
Type: Evergreen.
Height: 20–30 feet.

Conditions: Sun to partial shade. Prefers acidic, moist, well-drained soil.
Characteristics: Narrow, conical evergreen tree with small, glossy, very dark green leaves. A profusion of red fruit persists through winter. This tree has a delicacy and lightness of silhouette that other *Ilex* species lack. Self-pollinating.
Use: Specimen. Screening.

*Hybrid of *I. cassine* and *I. opaca.*

Ilex pedunculosa
(longstalk holly)

Early summer. See page 66.

Family: *Aquifoliaceae.*
Native Range: Japan, Korea.
USDA Zones: 4–8.
Type: Evergreen.
Height: 20–25 feet.

Conditions: Sun to light shade. Acidic, well-drained soil; will not tolerate alkaline soil. Needs open areas with good air circulation, since it is susceptible to leaf fungus.
Characteristics: Upright and loosely branched, with dark, lustrous laurel-like leaves. Bright red berries droop from long, slender stalks. Very hardy and adaptable.
Uses: Specimen. Screening.

Ilex verticillata 'Sparkleberry'*
(sparkleberry)

Mid-winter.

Mid-Autumn.

Family: *Aquifoliaceae.*
Native Range: Eastern North America.
USDA Zones: 3–9.
Type: Deciduous.
Height: 9 feet.

Conditions: Sun to partial shade. Acid, well-drained soil (tolerates alkaline p.H. soil to 8.0).
Characteristics: Multi-stemmed shrub with small yellow-green leaves and smooth grayish bark. Profuse display of brilliant red berry-like drupes, solitary or in pairs, which may persist into winter if not eaten by birds. Must have male graft or plant nearby for pollination.
Use: Massing. Specimen.

*Introduced by the United States National Arboretum.

Mahonia bealei
(leatherleaf mahonia)

Mid-summer. See page 212.

Family: *Berberidaceae.*
Native Range: China.
USDA Zone: 6.
Type: Evergreen.
Height: 10–12 feet.

Conditions: Sun to partial shade. Moist to average soil.
Characteristics: Coarse, spiny holly-like leaves colored a dull, dark green to blue-green. Light yellow, fragrant flowers in early spring with bluish-black sprays of grape-like fruits in summer.
Uses: Screening. Boundary control.

Magnolia virginiana*
(sweet bay magnolia)

Valerie Brown

Early summer. See page 83.

Family: *Magnoliaceae.*
Native Range: Eastern U.S., Texas Coast.
USDA Zones: 5–9.
Type: Deciduous.
Height: 10–20 feet.

Conditions: Sun or shade. Grows naturally in swampy woods, but also does well in sun. Fertile soil with liberal amounts of humus. Withstands dry conditions and raised planters.
Characteristics: Looks best as a multi-stemmed tree; allow some suckers to grow. Can reach 60 feet in warm climates, where foliage is winter-persistent. Leaves are 3–5 inches long, dark green above, whitish-gray below. The most fragrant *Magnolia* species. Small white flowers from early summer intermittently through early autumn.
Use: Specimen.

*Formerly *M. glauca.*

Nandina domestica
(heavenly bamboo)

Michael McKinley

Mid-Autumn. See page 172.

Family: *Berberidaceae.*
Native Range: Central China, Japan, India.
USDA Zones: 6–9.
Type: Evergreen.
Height: 6–8 feet.

Conditions: Sun to partial shade. Prefers fertile, moist, well-drained soil; will tolerate extremely dry and hot conditions. Slowly spreads from underground rhizomes. Needs mulch for winter protection.
Characteristics: Not a true bamboo. This member of the *Berberis* family has four-season interest. In spring, leaves are bronze to pink. White flower panicles bloom in early summer with delicate green foliage. Red berries appear in autumn as foliage turns bright red to scarlet, persisting into winter.
Use: Specimen. Accent. Small groupings. Screening.

Polygonum aubertii
(silver fleecevine)

Pamela Harper

Late summer. See page 223.

Family: *Polygonaceae.*
Native Range: Western China.
USDA Zones: 4–7.
Type: Deciduous.
Height: 25–35 feet.

Conditions: Sun to partial shade. Tolerates wide range of soil conditions and drought.
Characteristics: Light green foliage, sheathed with a multitude of fragrant white-to-greenish-white flower panicles from mid-summer to frost. Vigorous, fast-growing and extremely adaptable.
Use: Fences, walls, arbors and treillage.

Stranvaesia davidiana undulata
(Chinese stranvaesia)

Late winter.

Family: *Rosaceae.*
Native Range: West China.
USDA Zones: 6–8.
Type: Evergreen, winter-persistent.
Height: 16–20 feet.

Conditions: Sun to partial shade.
Fertile, slightly acid, moist soil.
Characteristics: Wide-spreading and vigorous habit; typically shrub-form.
Dark green foliage, with a bronze to purplish tinge. Small white flowers in terminal clusters appear in early summer. Scarlet red fruits peak in early winter, resistant to birds.
Use: Accents.

Viburnum x *pragense**
(Prague viburnum)

Mid-spring.

Family: *Caprifoliaceae.*
Native Range: China.
USDA Zones: 5–8.
Type: Evergreen.
Height: 10 feet.

Conditions: Sun to partial shade.
Prefers good drainage. **Characteristics:**
Extremely hardy. Lustrous, dark green leaves. Pink flower buds opening to creamy-white in mid-spring.
Use: Massing. Screening. Hedge.
Specimen.

*Hybrid of *V. rhytidophyllum* x *V. utile.*
Other notable species include
rhytidiphyllum, prunifolium, mariesii, setigerum.

Zelkova serrata 'Greenvase'*
(Japanese zelkova)

Late summer. See page 130.

Family: *Ulmaceae.*
Native Range: Japan.
USDA Zones: 5–8.
Type: Deciduous.
Height: 40–50 feet.

Conditions: Sun to partial shade.
Clayey to average soils. Tolerates wind, drought, air pollution and soil compaction. Highly resistant to Dutch elm disease; often recommended as a replacement for *Ulmus americana* (American elm).
Characteristics: Graceful, vase-shaped tree with many upright, arching branches. Foliage is dark green in summer, turning to yellow, orange, brown or burgundy in autumn.
Interesting grayed buff bark with a horizontal orange marking, exfoliating with age.
Use: Specimen. Shade. Street tree.

*Introduced by Princeton Nurseries, Princeton, New Jersey.

Selected Chronology

1965	The Vollmer Garden Baltimore, Maryland	Lonnie Joe Edwards, Sculptor John Seymour, Sculptor
1976	The Nef Garden Washington, D.C.	Grace Knowlton, Sculptor Marc Chagall, Artist
1977	The van Sweden Garden Washington, D.C.	Grace Knowlton, Sculptor
1978	The Hay Garden Washington, D.C.	Maija Hay, Potter
	The Taylor Garden Washington, D.C.	
1979	The Federal Reserve Landscape (Second Stage) The Board of Governors of the Federal Reserve System Washington, D.C.	George E. Patton, Inc., Landscape Architect (First Stage) Raya Bodnarchuk, Sculptor Sol Lewitt, Sculptor
	Showcase House Garden Westinghouse Communities of Naples, Inc. Naples, Florida	Robert E. Forsythe, Architect Holland Salley Interiors, Inc.
	The Woodward Garden Washington, D.C.	Antony Childs, Interior Designer
1980	The Turner Garden Naples, Florida	
1981	The Draper Garden Washington, D.C.	Thomas J. Stohlman, Architect
	The Anne Lloyd Garden Washington, D.C.	
1982	The Littlefield Garden Alexandria, Virginia	Pamela Heyne, Architect
	The Evelyn Nef Office Garden Washington, D.C.	Hugh Newell Jacobsen, Architect
	"Sculpture Returns to the Garden" Alex Rosenberg Gallery New York, New York	Lila Katzen, Sculptor
	The Sheffield Garden Washington, D.C.	Curtis Ripley, Potter

1983	The Bennett/Born Garden Washington, D.C.	
	The Gratz Garden Baltimore, Maryland	
	The Rosenberg Garden Water Mill, New York	Buffy Johnson, Artist
	The Smith Garden Washington, D.C.	Pamela Heyne, Architect
1984	The Evans Garden Washington, D.C.	Wiebenson & McInturff, Architects

	Freedom Plaza Planting Design
	Pennsylvania Avenue Development
	  Corporation
	Washington, D.C.
		George E. Patton, Inc., Landscape
		  Architect
		Venturi, Scott Brown and Associates,
		  Inc., Architects

1985	The Schneiderman Garden Washington, D.C.	Fisher/Gordon, Architects Antony Childs, Interior Designer
1986	A Georgetown Garden Washington, D.C.	Sandra Youssef Clinton, Project Landscape Architect Barbara Smith Herzberg, Sculptor
	Hillside Collage Potomac, Maryland	Sandra Youssef Clinton, Project Landscape Architect Harris Design Group, Architects
	The International Center The United States Department of State Washington, D.C.	MMM Design Group, Engineers
	The New American Garden The United States National Arboretum Washington, D.C.	John Cavanaugh, Sculptor
	The Platt Garden Washington, D.C.	Sandra Youssef Clinton, Project Landscape Architect
1987	An Apartment Terrace Washington, D.C.	Eric D. Groft, Project Landscape Architect Gerald Luss and Associates, Architects

	The Jacobs Garden
	  (Second Stage)
	Washington, D.C.
		Sandra Youssef Clinton, Project
		  Landscape Architect
		Lester Collins, Landscape Architect
		  (First Stage)
		Francis D. Lethbridge and Associates
		  P.C., Architects

	The German-American Friendship
	  Garden
	Presidential Commission for the
	  German-American Tricentennial
	Washington, D.C.
		Sandra Youssef Clinton, Project
		  Landscape Architect
		Leo A. Daly, Engineers

	The Slifka Garden Sagaponock, New York	Eric D. Groft, Project Landscape Architect Zwirko & Ortmann Architects, P.C. Arthur Smith, Interior Designer Hilda Steckel, Sculptor

Morrill Hall Plaza University of Minnesota St. Paul, Minnesota	Lawrence V. Frank, Project Landscape Architect Charles Wood, Landscape Architect Setter, Leach and Lindstrom Architects and Engineers
Northrop Plaza Planting Design University of Minnesota St. Paul, Minnesota	Lawrence V. Frank, Project Landscape Architect
1988 The Gelman Garden Chevy Chase, Maryland	Lawrence V. Frank, Project Landscape Architect Muse-Wiedemann, Architects
The Littlefield Garden Washington, D.C.	Sandra Youssef Clinton, Project Landscape Architect
Major General George Gordon Meade Monument Planting Design Pennsylvania Avenue Development Corporation Washington, D.C.	Charles A. Grafly, Sculptor
The Offutt Garden Upperco, Maryland	Eric D. Groft, Project Landscape Architect Nancy Watkins Denig, Landscape Architect
The Rosenberg Terrace Garden New York, New York	Sandra Youssef Clinton, Project Landscape Architect Andrée Putman, Interior Designer David Jacobs, Sculptor Henry Moore, Sculptor
The Shockey Garden Winchester, Virginia	Eric D. Groft, Project Landscape Architect
Chevy Chase Garden Plaza Chevy Chase Savings Bank, F.S.B. Bethesda, Maryland	Lawrence V. Frank, Project Landscape Architect Leo A. Daly, Architects and Engineers Martin Puryear, Sculptor

SELECTED WORKS IN PROGRESS

PRIVATE GARDENS

Glaubiger San Francisco, California	Peddy Phoenix, Maryland
Kauffman Camp Hill, Pennsylvania	Rossotti Washington, D.C.
Malcolm Greenwich, Connecticut	Ulfelder McLean, Virginia
Meyer Harbert, Michigan	Woodard Beaverkill Valley, New York
Bedell/Mills Shelter Island, New York	

PUBLIC AND COMMERCIAL LANDSCAPES

Alexander House Apartments
Silver Spring, Maryland

Americana Shopping Center
Manhassett, New York

Augusta National Golf Club
Augusta, Georgia

The Francis Scott Key Memorial Park
Washington, D.C.

Hester Industries, Inc.
Winchester, Virginia

The Lincoln Park Zoo
Chicago, Illinois

North Park, Battery Park City
New York, New York

The Palisades Mixed-Use Development
Arlington, Virginia

Parkside Housing Development
Washington, D.C.

Rock Rim Ponds Residential
Development
Pound Ridge, New York

Smith Property Development
Delaware County, Ohio

1. Sir Geoffrey Jellicoe and Susan Jellicoe, consultant eds.; Patrick Goode and Michael Lancaster, exec. eds., *Oxford Companion to Garden History.* (New York: Oxford University Press, 1986), p. 191.

2. James van Sweden still has this book in his collection: Faulkner, Ziegfeld, and Hill, *Art Today,* revised ed. (New York: Henry Holt & Co., 1953).

3. Frederick Steiner, "Dutch Master: Nico de Jonge," *Landscape Architecture* 79 (August 1989), p. 77.

4. This term has been much bandied about, and is only the latest in a list of labels which writers have sought to affix to the Oehme and van Sweden style, including "The Laissez-Faire Garden," "The New Romantic Garden," and "The Four Seasons Garden." However, "The New American Garden" seems to have caught on for an entire movement rather loosely defined. As such, it has sparked controversy. Some critics find the term "jingoistic"; others wish to judge its exponents by the number of native plants employed.

Although Allen Lacy has used the term as a jumping off point in "The Facts About . . . The New American Garden," *Vis à Vis* 3 (May 1989), p. 34, and "A New Influence in Gardens," *The New York Times Magazine* (October 16, 1988), p. 12, he says it is not entirely apropos, considering Oehme's and van Sweden's European educations and influences. But according to Charles Fenyvesi in "The Four-Season Garden," *The Washington Post,* (February 20, 1986), p. 28, ". . . their landscaping is recognized by horticulturists as being emphatically American." Fenyvesi enlarges on that point in "A Landscape Revolution," *Washington Post* (May 26, 1988), p. 22, saying that ". . . they have created a new American garden style."

As Elvin MacDonald has pointed out, in "The Cutting Edge," *Plants & Gardens News* 3, "The only official New American Garden on record is at the United States National Arboretum," so named and dedicated by Dr. H. Marc Cathey in 1986. Carole Ottesen's *The New American Garden* presents the following definition: "American-style gardens brim with soft, full, relaxed—often wild—plantings that complement the local landscape, adapt to regional growing conditions, and respond to seasonal change." (New York: Macmillan Publishing Company, 1987, p. 1.)

Other definitions include Graham Rose's ". . . gardens in which grasses predominate" in "Super Grasses Make a Welcome Comeback," in *The Sunday Times,* (London: August 7, 1988), p. 34, and Mac Griswold's "A dream of the lost prairies or whatever wild lost place each of us imagines," in "Garden Grasses," in *House and Garden* 160 (June 1988), p. 132.

The term is most usefully applied to the Oehme and van Sweden canon when it describes a landscape design that joins the casual American spirit with a melting pot of plants and ideas from across the world, East and West. Its *ideal* is the freedom and ease of the meadow. As James van Sweden wrote in a letter to the editor (*The Washington Post,* June 2, 1988), "Can anyone take seriously a suggestion that we return to the plant palette existing before Columbus and tell American garden designers past and present that combinations of imports and natives as seen in their gardens for hundreds of years are 'contrived'? . . . . Mother Nature has supplemented our fine American plant list with a magnificent collection of plants chosen from the rest of the world. Gardening is one aspect of international life in which peace and exchange exist freely." For this reason, we have subtitled this book, "New World Gardens."

5. Sir Geoffrey Jellicoe, et. al, *Oxford Companion to Garden History,* p. 492. This 635-page volume is an indispensable survey of the subject, including definitive entries on more than 700 gardens, as well as individuals, national histories, and terminology, written by expert contributors.

6. Karl Foerster, *Einzug der Gräser und Farne in die Garten,* 7th ed. (Stuttgart: Eugen Ulmer GmbH & Co., 1988), p. 11.

7. Author's notes, Landscape Architecture Foundation lecture given by Roberto Burle Marx, October 15, 1989, Cincinnati, Ohio.

8. Conversations with Roberto Burle Marx, as noted by Barbara Woodward, in Rio de Janeiro, Brasil, 1987.

9. Longwood Gardens, developed by Pierre S. du Pont, is a premier 20th-century American estate, with numerous exterior and conservatory gardens. Now open to the public, Longwood has become a leading research and educational institution offering degree, certificate and continuing education programs. The address is P.O. Box 501, Kennett Square, PA 19348-0501; telephone (215) 388-6741.

10. Janet Draper propagated *Senecio doria* at Kurt Bluemel's nursery in Baltimore, Maryland, in sufficient quantity for our design purposes.

11. A little-known way to control slug and snail damage is to mulch the crown of susceptible plants with "chicken grit"—a very coarse sand available at farmers' supply stores. The pests can't make their way across the particles, which measure up to ¼-inch in diameter.

Selected References

Ammann, Gustav. *Blühende Garten.* Stuttgart: Verlag Für Architektur, 1955.

Bailey, Liberty Hyde, and Bailey, E.Z.; *Hortus Third.* Revised by the Staff of the Liberty Hyde Bailey Hortorium, Cornell University. New York: Macmillan Publishing Co., 1976.

Baumann, Ernst. *Neue Gärten.* Zürich: Editions Girsbercier, 1955.

Bijhouwer, J.T.P. *Nederlandsche Tuinen En Buitenplaatsen.* Amsterdam: Allert de Lange, 1946.

Brookes, John. *The Garden Book.* New York: Crown Publishers, 1984.

Bye, A.E. *Art Into Landscape. Landscape Into Art.* Mesa, Ariz.: PDA Publishers, 1983.

Carpenter, Jot D., ed. *Handbook of Landscape Architecture Construction.* Washington, D.C.: Landscape Architecture Foundation, 1976.

Chatto, Beth. *The Dry Garden.* London: J. M. Dent & Sons, 1978.

Church, Thomas. *Gardens Are For People.* Second Edition. New York: McGraw-Hill Book Co., 1983.

Clouston, Brian. *Landscape Design with Plants.* London: Heinemann, 1977.

Crowe, Sylvia. *Garden Design.* New York: Heathside Press, 1959.

Dirr, Michael. *Manual of Woody Landscape Plants.* Champaign, Ill.: Stipes Publishing Co., 1975.

Douglas, William; Frey, Susan; Johnson, Norman K.; Littlefield, Susan; and Van Valkenburg, Michael. *Garden Design: History. Principles. Elements. Practice.* New York: Simon & Schuster, 1984.

Druse, Ken. *The Natural Garden.* New York: Clarkson N. Potter, 1989.

Eaton, Leonard K. *Landscape Artist in America.* Chicago: University of Chicago Press, 1964.

Eckbo, Garrett. *The Art of Home Landscaping.* New York: F. W. Dodge Corporation, 1956.

Foerster, Eva. *Ein Garten der Erinnerung.* Berlin: Union, 1982.

Foerster, Karl. *Einzug der Gräser and Farne in die Garten.* Seventh Edition. Stuttgart: Eugen Ulmer GmbH & Co., 1988.

Frederick, William H. *100 Great Garden Plants.* Portland: Timber Press, 1975.

Grounds, Roger. *Ornamental Grasses*. London: Pelham Books, Bas Printers, 1979.

Harper, Pamela, and McGourty, Frederick. *Perennials, How to Select and Grow*. Los Angeles: HP Books, 1984.

Hightshoe, Gary L. *Native Trees and Shrubs for Urban and Rural America*. New York: Van Nostrand Reinhold and Co., 1988.

Hobhouse, Penelope. *Garden Style*. Boston: Little, Brown and Co., 1988.

Itoh, Teiji. *The Gardens of Japan*. Tokyo: Kodasha International, 1984.

Jekyll, Gertrude. *Garden Ornament*. Second Edition. Woodbridge, England: Baron Publishing, 1982.

Jelitto, Leo; Schacht, Wilhelm; and Fessler, Alfred. *Die Freiland Schmuckstauden*. Stuttgart: Verlag Eugen Ulmer, 1950.

Jellicoe, Geoffrey, and Jellicoe, Susan. *The Landscape of Man: Shaping the Environment from Pre History to the Present*. New York: Thames & Hudson, 1987.

Le Corbusier. *New. World of Space*. New York: Reynal & Hitchcock, 1948.

Lloyd, Christopher. *Foliage Plants*. New York: Random House, 1973.

Masson, Georgina. *Italian Gardens*. New York: Harry N. Abrams, 1961.

Mattern, Hermann. *Garten Und Gartenlandschaften*. Stuttgart: Gerd Hatje, 1960.

McHarg, Ian. *Design With Nature*. New York: The Natural History Press, 1969.

Motta, Flavio L., *Roberto Burle Marx: e a nova visao da Paisagem*. Brasilia, Brasil: Livraria Nobel S.A., 1984.

Newman, Oscar. *Defensible Space*. New York: Macmillan Publishing Co., 1972.

Page, Russell. *The Education of a Gardener*. New York: Random House, 1983.

Plomin, Karl. *Der Vollendete Garten*. Stuttgart: Eugen Ulmer, 1975.

Poor, Janet M., with the Garden Club of America. *Plants That Merit Attention, Vol. I Trees*. Portland: Timber Press, 1984.

Rambach, Pierre, and Rambach, Susanne. *Gardens of Longevity in China and Japan*. New York: Rizzoli International Publications, 1987.

Simonds, John Ormsbee. *Landscape Architecture: A Manual of Site Planning*. Second Edition. New York: McGraw-Hill Book Company, 1984.

Spirn, Anne Whiston. *The Granite Garden: Urban Nature and Human Design*. New York: Basic Books, 1984.

Taylor, Norman. *Taylor's Guide to Ground Cover, Vines & Grasses*. Boston: Houghton Mifflin Company, 1986.

Taylor, Norman. *Taylor's Guide to Perennials*. Boston: Houghton Mifflin Company, 1986.

Thacker, Christopher. *The History of Gardens*. Berkeley, Calif.: University of California Press, 1979.

Tunnard, Christopher, and Pushkarev, Boris. *Man-Made America: Chaos or Control?* New Haven: Yale University Press, 1963.

Valentien, Otto. *Gärten*. Tübingen: Ernst Wasmuth, 1954.

Wilkinson, Elizabeth, and Henderson, Marjorie. *House of Boughs*. New York: Viking, Yolla Bally Press, 1985.

Wyman, Donald. *Wyman's Gardening Encyclopedia*. New York: MacMillan Publishing Co., 1971.

Photography and Production Credits

PHOTOGRAPHY
Rhoda Baer: 14, 156

Jonathan Blair: 282

Valerie Brown: 83, 111, 168–169, 170, 219, 235, 244, 274, 292

Ken Druse: 179, 182–183, 187, 263

Paul C. De Georges: 242

Henry Groskinsky: 72

Pamela Harper: 272, 274, 275, 278, 279, 289, 290, 292, 293

Jerry Harpur: 227

Carol M. Highsmith: 140

Saxon Holt: 249

Peter Jones: 120, 121, 122–123, 124, 174, 175, 187

Michael McKinley: front cover, endpapers, 2–3, 4, 10, 53, 54, 61, 66, 67, 68, 69, 70, 73, 74, 82, 84, 86, 89, 92, 93, 94, 97, 98, 99, 103, 105, 106, 107, 108, 109, 110, 112–113, 116, 117, 118–119, 126–127, 129, 130, 137, 139, 141, 142, 143, 146, 147, 148, 150–151, 152–153, 157, 158, 159, 160, 163, 164, 172, 173, 178, 186, 187, 190, 191, 192, 193, 194, 196, 197, 198, 200, 202, 203, 207, 208, 216, 218, 220, 228, 233, 239, 241, 243, 245, 250, 251, 252, 253, 255, 257, 260, 265, 266–267, 273, 274, 275, 276, 277, 278, 279, 280, 281, 283, 284, 285, 286, 287, 288, 289, 290, 291, 292

John Neubauer: 45, 58, 78, 79, 80, 104, 134–135, 138, 176, 210, 212, 214, 215, 223, 246, 248, 254, 277

Bradley Olman: 1, 64

Marina Schinz: 180–181

Caroline Segui-Kosar: back cover, 100–101, 144–145, 204–205, 272, 275

Michael Selig: 155, 217

Gretchen Tatje: 62

Volkmar Wentzel: 77, 91, 114–115, 128, 132–133, 166, 167, 224–225, 231, 238, 241, 247, 262, 274, 281, 286, 288

Cynthia Woodyard: 291

COORDINATION
Sandra Youssef Clinton

PHOTOGRAPHY EDITING
Michael McKinley
Caroline Segui-Kosar

CHRONOLOGY AND BIBLIOGRAPHY RESEARCH
Lisa E. Delplace

DRAFTING
Site Plans — René M. Albacete

Planting Plans and Sections—
Sharon Bradley-Papp

Perspectives—Jeffrey A. Charlesworth

Details—Lisa E. Delplace

GLOSSARY RESEARCH
Bruce J. Riddell

ADMINISTRATIVE ASSISTANCE
Ann M. Hatsis
Susan L. Stone
Monica L. Lollar

Credit is also due to current and former employees, not previously listed, who have contributed to the work shown in this book.

Sheila Brady
Joseph Ferrara
Brian Katen
Sunny Jung Scully
Mary Villarejo
Benedikt Wasmuth